*L*OVEMAN'S

Meet Me Under the Clock

TIM HOLLIS

Charleston   London

THE
History
PRESS

Published by The History Press
Charleston, SC 29403
www.historypress.net

Copyright © 2012 by Tim Hollis
All rights reserved

First published 2012

Manufactured in the United States

ISBN 978.1.60949.342.4

Library of Congress CIP data applied for.

CONTENTS

Acknowledgements

S ince whatever existed of a Loveman's archive was scattered far and wide after the stores closed in 1980, the information contained in this book had to be gathered from many different sources. Several departments of the Birmingham Public Library, including the Archives and Southern History Collections, contain one-of-a-kind relics from Loveman's long history. Surviving descendants of A.B. Loveman's children were also helpful in locating information about the family. In alphabetical order, these are the individuals most responsible for the book existing in its present form:

Harold Apolinsky
Jim Baggett, Birmingham Public Library Archives
Don Blumenthal
Morris Blumenthal Jr.
Teeny Brannon
Bruce Brasseale, McWane Science Center
Marion Breyer
Grady and Sharon Burrow
Del "Twinkles" Chambordon
Nicholas Cobbs
Miriam Cohn
Eleanor Cunningham
Rebecca Dobrinski
Liz Ellaby, Birmingham-Jefferson History Museum
Jack Farber

ACKNOWLEDGEMENTS

Martha Fowler
Lance George
Peggy Hirsch Greenwald
Cliff and Ann Holman
Dolores Hydock
Kelly Kazek
David Kern
Ann Langford
Ernest Langner, Dixie Neon
Angelique LeDoux
J.T. Legg
John Lehman
David Robertson
Robert Roden
Scott Seligman
Jerry Sklar
Lamar Smith, McWane Science Center
Jack Thomas Jr.

Chapter 1

THE MAN CALLED LOVEMAN

For almost a century, from 1887 to 1980, one of Birmingham's most renowned and respected retailers was Loveman's. Now, when it comes to the history of this venerable institution, reasons directly related to the passage of time obviously dictate that the second fifty years of that impressive business life are much easier to document than the first fifty. With that thought in mind, let us begin by delving into some dusty records and crumbling newspapers and see just how much we can learn.

This much is certain: Loveman's was founded by an immigrant named Adolph Bernard Loveman, usually referred to simply as A.B. Inasmuch as the details of his early life go back approximately 160 years, it is understandable that no living person can claim to have firsthand knowledge of the subject. However, thanks to some impressive genealogical research by family historian Scott Seligman, at least we have some idea as to how A.B. Loveman came to the United States.

First, we must address the subject of A.B.'s last name. According to Seligman, the original family name was Liebman. Just where the family originated seems difficult to ascertain because national borders have changed so much since those days, but Seligman writes:

> Jewish settlement in Slovakia dates to the 11th century, but the earliest surviving records of a Liebman family in the Zemplen region—traditionally part of Hungary but today split between northern Hungary and eastern Slovakia—date only to the 19th century. Birth records can be found from as far back as 1840, and the 1869 Austro-Hungarian census, which survives for the Zemplen region, is a particularly rich source. It enumerates several Liebman families living in and around the town of Zamutov at the time.

This handsome portrait of A.B. Loveman was one of the most often-reproduced images of the founder of the store bearing his name, but its exact year of origin is unknown. *Robert Roden collection.*

Yes, Adolph Bernard Liebman was one of those. Born in 1844, he is said to have spent the first twenty-one years of his life as a farmer and shepherd in that rural Hungarian countryside. The years immediately following the American Civil War saw, for some reason, a mass exodus of Liebmans from Europe to the United States, and A.B. also made his way across the big pond. Seligman's research shows that this branch of the family, which Americanized the spelling of the name from Liebman to Loveman, passed through Michigan and Ohio before penetrating deep into the defeated former Confederate States.

It was apparently in 1865 that A.B. Loveman arrived on American shores, but there is no real story to explain how he made the transition from being a farmer in Europe to becoming a door-to-door peddler in the South. Perhaps the correct answer is the simplest one: it was one of the relatively few jobs available for Jewish immigrants in those days. Whatever the circumstances, A.B. is said to have spent some time in Pulaski, Tennessee, before venturing into Alabama and settling in Greensboro, south of Tuscaloosa. (You may ask why he did not instead head for a more urban location such as Birmingham. Simple: Birmingham did not yet exist in 1870, the year A.B. set up shop in Greensboro.)

In 1984, Greensboro native Lucia May set down some of the recollections she remembered hearing from the old-timers when she was growing up there:

> *Many years ago, a Jewish foot-peddler trudged into town at intervals. The households where he displayed his wares welcomed him heartily and sometimes served refreshments. Someone would give him lodging for the*

night, free of charge. He never forgot Greensboro and its people. Finally, he founded a store in Birmingham that eventually became the city's largest and finest department store. In later years, his son, who became president of the company, loved to give a job to anyone who came from Greensboro.

Another momentous event that took place for A.B. in 1870 was his marriage to the former Minnie Weil. This and beginning what was to become a successful Greensboro dry goods store would have been enough to occupy just about anyone, but within a few years, the abovementioned son had joined the family. Now this is where the waters get murky again. Although Joseph Loveman was never known to the public as anything other than A.B.'s biological son, Joseph was actually born Joseph Weil and was the son of Minnie's sister. Under circumstances known only to the family, Joseph was legally adopted by his uncle A.B., took the Loveman surname and, in the future, would perhaps have more influence over the store bearing that name than even the founder.

The Greensboro years of Loveman's are difficult to document with any certainty, although local historians can still point out the location of the long-demolished family home and the corner where the original store stood. Unfortunately, that particular block in downtown Greensboro burned to the ground in 1902, so like those who knew A.B. personally, there is no person alive who can be said to have seen the original building except in faded photographs. After the block was rebuilt the following year, the store on the corner occupied by the original Loveman's went through many different

For many years, this photo was purported to be A.B. Loveman's first store in Birmingham. Subsequent research, however, has proven that it is actually his Greensboro store, which operated from 1870 to 1887. *Del Chambordon collection.*

occupants. In one of those odd twists of fate, it eventually ended up as an outlet of Birmingham-based dime store chain V.J. Elmore, whose signage still exists on the aged structure.

The story becomes only slightly more documented beginning in 1887. After seventeen successful years in Greensboro, the Loveman family pulled up stakes and moved to Birmingham, which at that time was only sixteen years old. A.B. left his Greensboro store in the capable hands of one of his wife's family members, Dave Weil, under whose control it flourished for many more years. Again, there seems to be nothing to indicate just why this action was taken, but by 1887, Birmingham was getting out of some of its earliest growing pains, and it is likely that A.B. Loveman saw it as a market just waiting to be tapped into.

Tradition holds that the first A.B. Loveman Dry Goods Emporium opened at 1915 Second Avenue North in early May 1887. (That site, for those old enough to remember it, later became the location for the Strand Theater, one of Birmingham's early, lavish silent movie houses.) Within a month of opening the store, Loveman had taken on a partner. This was Moses V. Joseph, and pretty much all we know about his pre-Loveman's career is what was published in his obituary:

> *An Alabamian all the way through, Mr. Joseph was born in Greensboro in 1859, the son of J. and Rachael Terquem Joseph. He moved at an early age with his parents to Mobile, where he attended the old Barton Academy. His father, like most of the Southern men who fought for the Confederacy, had to begin life anew after the war, and Mr. Joseph did not have the opportunity of completing his education. At 13 years of age he started out to make a living for himself.*
>
> *He left Mobile and went to Demopolis, where he became a clerk in his brother-in-law's mercantile store. The ruling desire of his boyhood was to become a merchant like his father before him, and establish a business that would be among the leading firms of the South. From Demopolis, Mr. Joseph went to Selma and became employed by the old established firm of Obendorf and Ulman, and worked up from cash boy to general manager of the firm.*

The article goes on to state that Moses Joseph and A.B. Loveman had developed a warm personal friendship, and once the new Loveman store in Birmingham was established, A.B. sent for Moses to come join him. We can only assume that they got to know each other during Joseph's time in

Only weeks after setting up shop in Birmingham, Loveman took on a partner in the person of Moses V. Joseph. *Birmingham Public Library Archives Portrait collection.*

Demopolis and Selma, and Joseph having family roots in Greensboro only added to their association with each other.

Under normal circumstances, we would be able to more accurately document when all of this took place by consulting the issues of the Birmingham newspapers preserved on microfilm. However, there is a glitch: for newspapers to be microfilmed, they had to survive in the first place, and the vast majority of them from the 1880s did not. The earliest surviving Loveman's ad is from July 21, 1887, and it confirms that the store's name had already become Loveman & Joseph by that early date.

What happened next is perhaps even more of a mystery than how Loveman and Joseph came to be associated with each other. Somehow or other, in either January or February 1889, they took on a third partner in the store, Emil Loeb. The official company name then became Loveman, Joseph & Loeb, which it would remain until the 1950s. Very, very little is known about Emil Loeb except that he was born in Germany in 1864 and immigrated to the United States in 1881 at the age of seventeen. It also seems that he spent very little time in Birmingham, remaining primarily a New Yorker. Just how or why Loveman and Joseph agreed to such a comparatively young

This is the earliest existing ad for the newly established Birmingham firm of Loveman & Joseph, from July 1887. *Author's collection.*

(and largely absentee) partner may never be known, but Loeb must have had some quality they could discern.

Whatever the case, apparently the team of Loveman, Joseph & Loeb had all the right chemistry because by 1891 the store had outgrown the Second Avenue site. For a reported sum of $41,000, the company purchased a lot fronting on Nineteenth Street, about halfway between Second and Third Avenues. On the south, it was adjoined by the Florence Hotel and on the north by a brick structure known as the Elyton Block. The four-story building that was erected on this site was indeed a sight to see in nineteenth-century Birmingham, and upon its grand opening on September 3, an anonymous newspaper writer fairly grasped for superlatives to describe it:

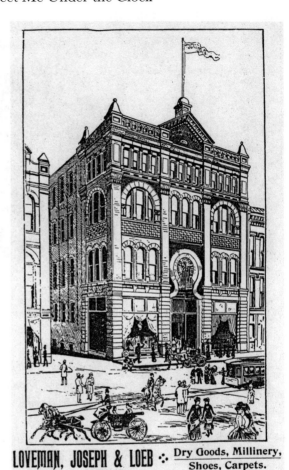

In 1891, Loveman, Joseph & Loeb moved into its new home, an ornate four-story structure fronting on Nineteenth Street. *Author's collection.*

One enters a touring arch and finds himself in a vestibule inlaid with mosaics of colored marble. In front, the firm name stands out in bold-lettered relief, and within the crescent made by the triad, a brilliant star shoots forth rays telling of past success and presaging future prosperity. The doors are heavy grained oak, solid and massive.

Inside one sees long rows of counters neatly and conveniently arranged, large passages between and seats for customers every few feet apart. Passing to the rear of the first floor, there is found upon the right a passenger elevator, dumb-waiter for sending goods up and down and a set of speaking tubes to communicate with every floor.

Upon the second floor are the upholstery, carpet, wallpaper and millinery departments. The female employees have here attached their cloak rooms,

13

It appears the entire staff and management of Loveman, Joseph & Loeb assembled in front of the massive main entrance for this 1891 opening day photo. *Rebecca Dobrinski collection.*

dining room, etc. The third and fourth floors will be devoted to the wholesale department, constantly growing. A square opening in each floor gives an abundance of light and adds to the convenience.

Only eight years later, another expansion was in the works, and it was this one that gave the store the footprint with which most Birminghamians are familiar. For $50,000, Loveman, Joseph & Loeb purchased the Elyton Block and in March 1899 began demolition to make way for what the newspapers termed a "double building." What that meant was that the Loveman, Joseph & Loeb building would now extend north all the way to Third Avenue, and the entire structure would occupy approximately a quarter of the city block in which it sat.

In an article that took up most of a page on March 14, 1899, the newspaper writer claimed that through its mail-order department, Loveman, Joseph & Loeb had become famous throughout the South. In fact, a mural painted on the western wall of the new four-story addition proudly proclaimed the store as the "largest south of the Ohio." With all the hype, it is somewhat surprising that the completion of the new addition did not attract more newspaper space when it was completed that fall; ads simply referred to it as "the annex," as the original building still contained the main entrance.

The articles of the period do give some insight into how the three business partners divided up their daily chores. "Emil Loeb is the New York resident

In 1899, Loveman, Joseph & Loeb completed construction of an annex that enlarged the store to take up almost a quarter of the city block in which it sat. *Rebecca Dobrinski collection.*

buyer, spending ten months of every twelve in that city," the reporter explained. "The business man of the firm is M.V. Joseph. He has no superior in the south in the position he occupies with the firm and in its touch with the public." Somewhat oddly, the founder of the company received the briefest description: "Mr. Loveman devotes himself to the general supervision of the entire house."

Perhaps A.B. Loveman's attention was somewhat divided by the imposing new South Highlands home he was having built for himself and his family at 8 Fairview Circle, on the slope of Red Mountain. (The street is today known as Rhodes Circle.) By that time, there were four children in the family; besides Joseph Loveman, there were daughters Esther and Leona and another son, Berney. The new Loveman home was amazing to behold and remains so today.

About the time the new house was finished, the Lovemans hired a new cook, Rosie Gaston. Sharing living space with her in the servants' quarters behind the home was Rosie's young son, Arthur. During those years of living in such close proximity with the Lovemans, Arthur became inseparable

Around 1900, A.B. Loveman and his family moved into their imposing new home on what is today Rhodes Circle. *Robert Roden collection.*

friends with Berney, as the two were almost exactly the same age. There are numerous stories about Arthur and Berney spending almost all their waking time with each other, sometimes venturing to a nearby creek to watch baptisms and dare each other to furtively "chunk hickory nuts at the preacher." It is obvious that Arthur not only made friends that crossed racial barriers at the time but also must have picked up some tips on how to run a business, because A.G. Gaston eventually became Birmingham's most successful African American businessman in an era when there were considerably more obstacles in the way of such a goal than there would be today. As for Berney Loveman, his life took a less happy turn. At the age of twenty-five, on October 31, 1917, Berney threw himself out of an eighth-floor hotel window in New York City. The reason? He was despondent over not being allowed to marry his fiancée.

By 1900, there was no doubt that Loveman, Joseph & Loeb was the leading department store (or dry goods store, as it was usually called) in Birmingham, but it probably deserves mention here that other branches of the Loveman family had settled in Nashville and Chattanooga, and with apparently no communication having taken place between them, they, too, went into the dry goods/department store business. Loveman's of Chattanooga was probably the more famous of these "other Loveman's,"

This portrait of the entire Loveman family was probably made around 1896, judging from the ages of the individuals. A.B. and Minnie Loveman are pictured with sons Joseph and Berney and daughters Esther and Leona. Inasmuch as A.B. was stated as having only four children at the time of his death in 1916, the identity of the third girl in this photo is a mystery. *Robert Roden collection.*

as citizens of Birmingham considered them, and eventually the market area for the Tennessee and Alabama chains would somewhat overlap and cause occasional confusion. What is even more confusing, though, is a set of newspaper ads that appeared in September 1899, just as the newly enlarged Loveman, Joseph & Loeb building was being completed. Somehow, during that period, Birmingham had another store known as Loveman, Jaros and Co. Although it was advertised as "the Trade Palace of Second Avenue," surviving members of the Loveman family disavow any knowledge of its existence or origin or what part of the family was associated with it. In the long run, Loveman, Jaros and Co. must have had a short run, as its name has been all but erased from Birmingham's retail history.

In 1913, for reasons unknown, Emil Loeb decided to retire from the department store business. In what seems like a most unusual move, he then took a position with the Coplay Cement Manufacturing Company in Coplay, Pennsylvania, and remained with that enterprise until shortly before his death in 1941. There would be a succession of other people named Loeb associated with Loveman, Joseph & Loeb over the next several years, but what, if any, familial relationship they had with Emil has been impossible to determine.

If Emil Loeb ever returned to Birmingham for visits during his years in the cement manufacturing trade, he would have found it difficult to recognize the store he had helped establish. On July 3, 1916, Loveman, Joseph & Loeb again made front-page headlines by announcing that it was about to expand once more. By that time, what had formerly been considered the 1899 "annex" was now part of the entire store, and it was time to build a new six-story annex fronting on Third Avenue. The announcement made much of the fact that the new addition would be of all steel construction—something that would have great significance many years in the future. The addition of the annex would also be the impetus for a remodeling of the entire Loveman, Joseph & Loeb building, "so extensive that practically a new building will be constructed."

Most visible from the outside would be a new limestone surfacing that would hide the old brick exterior. Also, since the parapets, balustrades and other ornamentation that had been so fashionable in the 1890s were now already looking antiquated, they would all be removed, and the remodeled Loveman, Joseph & Loeb would resemble a huge, rectangular white box. Departments would be shifted around as changing times had dictated; for example, the store office was moved from the mezzanine to the fourth floor, and its former space was devoted to selling phonographs.

In one of those strange historical juxtapositions, the very day after these major announcements was made, the front page again had store-related news but a much less happy story. On July 4, 1916, seventy-two-year-old A.B. Loveman died at his Fairview Circle home after what was described as a five-year illness, "two years of which had been alarming to his family." It was reported that his undisclosed illness had become critical during the preceding two weeks, "his death expected hourly." By that time, the family had become a bit more scattered than when the house was built. Daughter Esther was married and living in Little Rock, although she had returned to be at A.B.'s bedside at his death, and son Berney was serving in the Alabama National Guard and stationed in Montgomery. Leona was still living at home, and Joseph was living next door to the family residence in his own fine home built on a completely different architectural model than his father's.

The black-bordered advertisement that appeared in the *Birmingham News* the next day employed what now sounds like rather archaic, but extremely respectful, text and punctuation:

In the shadow of the Calamity which has befallen us we and our whole
House stand silent and uncovered.
Today we mourn the loss of our founder—Mr. A.B. Loveman.
As one outward expression of the profound regret we feel,
OUR STORE WILL BE CLOSED ALL DAY WEDNESDAY.

The loss of A.B. Loveman caused some restructuring in the store's management. Later in 1916, the following positions were listed: M.V. Joseph, president; Joseph H. Loveman, vice-president; Leo Loeb, second vice-president and general manager; M. Lenk, assistant treasurer; W.E. Hooper, secretary; and Leopold Loeb, assistant secretary. Once again, how or if Leo Loeb and Leopold Loeb (who were apparently two different people, perhaps father and son) were related to the recently departed Emil Loeb is a mystery.

All in all, 1916 was a remarkably eventful year in the store's neighborhood. That was also when the old Florence Hotel, Loveman, Joseph & Loeb's next-door neighbor to the south, was demolished and another retail showplace built in its place. This was an expansion of the long-established department store belonging to Louis Saks, up to that point located at the corner of Nineteenth Street and First Avenue. While the building would house several different enterprises over the years, it would eventually become critical in the preservation of Loveman's digs. You will just have to stick with us as we go along to find out why, though.

Chapter 2

CITY STORES
COMES TO TOWN

The dust had barely settled from the big remodeling project that was meant to bring the nineteenth-century Loveman, Joseph & Loeb building into the twentieth century. An event was about to take place that would not only graphically demonstrate the changing face of retail in America but would also have a dramatic effect on the store's future.

In the summer of 1923, a suitor came knocking on Loveman, Joseph & Loeb's massive front doors. That would-be Romeo was R.J. Goerke of Newark, New Jersey. Goerke was in the process of founding a new department store company he would call City Stores and was doing so by purchasing the controlling stock in what he determined to be the major retailers in their respective markets. Having made overtures to B. Lowenstein of Memphis and Maison Blanche ("White House") in New Orleans, Goerke wanted to put Birmingham in his bag by making the city's biggest store part of City Stores.

The deal went through, although just what sort of negotiations led up to it is vague after so many years. Loveman family lore has it that Joseph Loveman was on an out-of-town trip when Goerke came a-callin', and M.V. Joseph and Leo Loeb sold their interests in the store to him. When Loveman returned home, it was to the discovery that he was now a minority stockholder in his own father's store. It is impossible to know just how accurate that account may be, but at least that is how it has been told in the family for generations.

This news was not greeted by the general public any better than it reportedly was by Joseph Loveman. This was the period when chain stores of all types—from A&P and Piggly Wiggly supermarkets to drugstores such

The exact location of this baseball field is unknown, but Loveman, Joseph & Loeb was observing its thirty-fourth anniversary in 1921 by plastering the outfield with advertisements. *Rebecca Dobrinski collection.*

as Walgreen's and Rexall to five-and-tens such as F.W. Woolworth and J.J. Newberry to such restaurants as Howard Johnson's—were beginning their biggest encroachment yet on what had formerly been the turf of innumerable locally owned mom and pop–type businesses. Many people had an innate distrust of these companies that were run by far distant owners with no vested personal interest in each town except its ability to make profits. Humorist Will Rogers probably spoke for the majority when he quipped, "Chain stores are about as friendly as chain gangs."

Such was the thinking Goerke and his new City Stores company had to face when he came to Birmingham that August to meet with the most prominent businessmen in the area. Just the headline that appeared in the newspaper summed up everyone's worst fears: "L., J. & L. STORE TO KEEP INDIVIDUALITY" it screamed, with the subheading "Not One of 'Chain,' R.J. Goerke Tells Birmingham Business Men." In the article itself, Goerke was quoted as telling the assemblage, "The Loveman, Joseph & Loeb style will remain truly Birmingham. Being entirely convinced that the South has great progress ahead, I am certain that continued success will come to the present efficient organization of the company."

While these momentous events were taking place, Loveman's was gaining some new neighbors that would ultimately come to have varying degrees of influence on its future. In 1899, Louis Pizitz had arrived in Birmingham to

A major remodeling of Loveman, Joseph & Loeb in 1916 had removed most of the gaudy nineteenth-century ornamentation seen in the earlier photo and converted the store into a giant white box. *Rebecca Dobrinski collection.*

found his own dry goods business, but at the time, he was having enough trouble just keeping his enterprise going that Loveman, Joseph & Loeb likely did not even begin to consider him a competitor. That had changed by 1925, and the huge new Pizitz department store that rose a block away from the Loveman, Joseph & Loeb corner stood seven stories above the street, with an additional full basement that could be used for selling. From that time on, the two stores would be the Gimbel's and Macy's of Birmingham, each delighting the shopping public with its attempts to outshine the other.

Adjoining Loveman, Joseph & Loeb's six-story annex on Third Avenue, the magnificent Alabama Theatre was erected by the Paramount chain and opened the day after Christmas 1927. It, too, would have a long-standing relationship with its department store neighbor but generally a much more amicable one than Pizitz. We shall be hearing more from both of these relatively new arrivals in the pages to come.

Almost immediately after the purchase by City Stores, a gradual, at first almost imperceptible, change began to take place in the Loveman, Joseph

& Loeb advertising. Although the complete name continued to be used, more and more ads—especially in the fine print at first—began referring to the institution simply as Loveman's. No explanation was given for this drastic case of shorthand, but we can indulge in some pure speculation that likely hits somewhere close to the bull's-eye of truth.

One hint comes from a May 1929 newspaper article observing the store's forty-second anniversary. The first paragraph sheds some light on the mystery of the incredible shrinking name: "Loveman, Joseph & Loeb, one of the three oldest department stores in the city, Wednesday celebrated its 42nd anniversary. Loveman's, as everyone knows the firm, has grown with Birmingham, each year seeing a new development, a new expansion."

From this, it is easy to extrapolate that in all likelihood, the public began referring to Loveman, Joseph

Loveman-Joseph & Loeb
Birmingham, Ala.

This illustrated edition of *The Night Before Christmas* was most likely a 1920s giveaway from Loveman, Joseph & Loeb's toy department. Notice the erroneous hyphen between Loveman and Joseph. *Author's collection.*

& Loeb as Loveman's long before the store's publicity did. Such a move was certainly not unheard of in the trademark business. For decades, Coca-Cola tried to discourage people from referring to it by the abbreviated name "Coke," but when it became apparent that battle was already lost, the company gave in and in the 1940s registered "Coke" as an alternate name. In more recent years, McDonald's has had to contend with that slang nickname of uncertain origin, "Mickey D's." Instead of fighting it, the hamburger barons have registered that name as one of their own trademarks. It would

The January White Sale!

Upholds a tradition for fine qualities and low prices

—This is the psychological moment to make important additions to your lingerie supply, and to round out the completeness of your stock of bed and table linens. Prices are down. Qualities are traditionally fine, and values the best we've seen in years.

Partial list of specials in bedding:

Lingerie
Partial list of the special values

$5.00 crepe de chine silk gowns, $3.95.
—Tailored or frilly are these gowns of pastel tints and white. Lace trimming, tucks, ribbons and rosebuds adorn some styles. Excellent quality.

$1.98 hand made Philippine gowns, $1.00.
—Hand made and hand embroidered, these gowns of softest white fabric are splendid values for their long wear and daintiness.

French voile teddies special, $1.00.
—Sheer and fine are teddies of French voile in white and pastel shades. With lovely trimmings.

$2.98 Value French voile gowns, $1.98.
—Softly clinging are these exquisite gowns of delicately tinted French voile. Also in white. Tasteful trimmings.

$2.50 crepe de chine teddies and step-ins, $1.98.
—Pastel tints and white gleam in these lustrous teddies and step-ins, beautifully made and trimmed.

81x90 Sleepwell sheets, $1.14 each.
—Made of genuine Wearwell nine-quarter bleached sheeting. Torn and hemmed, ready for use. $1.39 quality.

All linen pillow cases, $3.50.
—Pure linen pillow cases are hand hemstitched and already laundered. Fine texture, smooth and firm.

Indian head pillow tubing, 25c yard.
—42 inch pillow tubing of genuine Indian head will make cases of the finest quality. Smooth linen finish.

81x105 striped bed spreads, $1.95.
—Seamless bed spreads with scalloped edges have fast color stripes of blue, rose, gold, heliotrope or green. Long enough to cover bolster.

Single bed sheets, 98c each.
—63x99 sheets for single bed are seamless and full bleached. Neatly hemmed. Extra long to tuck securely. Soft finish.

Partial list of specials in materials:

10 yard bolt long cloth, $1.59.
—Snow white longcloth has a soft chamois finish for making undergarments of finest quality. Closely woven.

36 inch pajama checks, 15c yard.
—Good heavy quality, suitable for making men's and boys' undergarments. Neat checks are woven into this firm yet flexible fabric.

27x27 hemmed diapers, $1.29 dozen.
—Torn and hemmed diapers, made from a selected cotton, are put up in sealed sanitary package, holding one dozen.

10 yard bolt Jap nainsook, $3.89.
—This well-known Jap-Nagasaki nainsook is especially fine for infant's wear. Made from one of the finest Egyptian yarns.

Mercerized English broadcloth, 39c yard.
—Highly mercerized English broadcloth is bleached white with a lustrous finish for making dresses and shirts. 36 inches wide.

LOVEMAN, JOSEPH & LOEB

Looking for a prime example of 1920s-style advertising art? Search no further than this flyer for Loveman, Joseph & Loeb's January 1928 "White Sale." It strongly resembles the style of newspaper comic strips of the day. *Birmingham Public Library Southern History collection.*

seem logical that Loveman's would have eventually picked up on the same type of colloquial usage of its own name.

It must be admitted that "Loveman's" was easier to say and promote than the full name. In fact, when "Loveman, Joseph & Loeb" was spelled out on a lighted sign that was mounted to the corner of the building, so many letters were involved that the sign extended almost the entire span of the four-story height of the edifice.

Perhaps it was just as well that Loveman's chose to embrace its new moniker, because during 1929, two other events took place that might have affected the situation. In the early months of that year, Leo Loeb resigned his position with the company. As we have already seen, Leo may or may not have been related to co-founder Emil Loeb, but at least he had maintained the family name on the board of directors. On May 4, Moses V. Joseph died at age seventy at his home at 2617 Highland Avenue. His obituary on the front page of the *Birmingham News* occupied more space than had A.B. Loveman's own obituary in 1916 and, as we saw in the last chapter, gave practically the only biographical information about him that is known to exist. Joseph Loveman was now president of the store, and the newspaper ads made a point of pride of including that information as part of their ongoing battle to not have Loveman's branded as a chain store. One of them read like this:

> *This store is affiliated with six other large stores (elsewhere in America) for the purpose of creating a supreme BUYING POWER. Loveman's, however, is operated and governed by Birmingham men and women, Most of them you know, through their long association with this store. With them, and because of them, "Loveman's" has attained its present place of eminence.*

The use of quotation marks around the Loveman's name (at least in one of its usages) indicates that it was still considered more or less a nickname at that point, but as the months and years went by, it would more and more come to replace the longer, more unwieldy logo.

By the time of this January 1929 newspaper ad, the store's advertising was beginning to refer to itself more and more often as simply "Loveman's." *Author's collection.*

Somewhat unexpectedly, in August 1931, Joseph Loveman announced that he was retiring from his position with the store bearing his name. No reason was given in the surviving newspaper coverage, although the lasting effects of the Great Depression that began in the closing months of 1929 might have had something to do with it. His position as store president was assumed by Edmund Goerke, nephew of the City Stores' owner. Needless to say, this turn of events probably did not do much to reassure those who were still suspicious of Loveman's outside ownership. In an editorial, the *News* opined:

> *Indubitably, through knowledge imparted by the elder Goerke, who has made frequent visits to Birmingham, the new local executive is by no means unfamiliar with conditions here. For while Birmingham is outwardly and visibly concerned essentially with business, primarily it is a big Southern country town with all the virtues and faults of the Old South.*

Whatever the reaction to his replacement, Joseph Loveman's "retirement" turned out to be a short one. In January 1932, he was appointed to the post of director in the national City Stores hierarchy, and in February 1932, he resumed the presidency of Loveman's with no questions asked. The store took out a full-page newspaper ad to trumpet this event, and the fine print makes it sound as if his "retirement" had not been entirely of his own choosing. Under gigantic letters reading "JOE LOVEMAN IS BACK," the ad elaborated:

> *That's the message that went winging throughout the store last Monday. Buyers whispered it to buyers, clerks told office workers, wrapping girls told it to the boyfriend in the shipping department. The whole store was buzzing like a beehive; there was laughter, good fellowship; everybody wanted to talk about it. Joe Loveman is back! Then they rushed to his office on the fourth floor to congratulate him. Work was suspended until they could welcome the Chief back home. Joe Loveman is back! Those words mean a lot to this store. Joe Loveman, the man who has given 32 years of his life—and he is still a young man—is back at his old desk, steering the good ship that was launched by his father back in the days when a plank walk led up 20th Street from the L&N Station. The aims and ideals and policies and ambitions of A.B. Loveman and M.V. Joseph came on down through the years, perpetuated by Joe Loveman, the son.*
>
> *Then the business was sold into a chain store system. Joe Loveman continued to be head of the store until last August when he stepped out. A lot of water has gone over the dam in the last few years; a lot of changes*

In this rare view of the store's exterior Christmas decorations, circa 1930, notice that the vertical sign bearing the entire Loveman, Joseph & Loeb name had to be almost as tall as the four-story building to get all the letters in. *Author's collection.*

were made in this store; many things have happened since last August. But Joe Loveman is back! New executives are at the head of the company that owns Loveman, Joseph & Loeb, and they have put Joe Loveman back at the head of this business.

Yes, in case anyone missed it, Joseph Loveman was back, and his employees were happy to have him. When the store celebrated its customary anniversary, its forty-sixth, in May 1933, no one could have foreseen what was going to happen before it reached its next one. Had Joseph Loveman, with his deep family ties, not been restored to the office of presidency, it might well have been the end of the story.

Chapter 3

A Hot Time
Downtown Tonight

On Friday, March 9, 1934, Loveman's took out a huge double-page spread in the *Birmingham News*, entreating readers to "Come to Loveman's Easter Party Tomorrow." Among artwork of bunnies, eggs and Easter lilies, the subheading touted March 10 as "an all-important day for seeing and buying spring apparel and accessories, styled right and priced right!"

From a twenty-first-century perspective, there was no doubt about the "priced right" part of that claim. Ladies' "Suits! Coats! Dresses! In a beauty of quality that is typical of Loveman!" could be had for $17.50. Spring dresses were $7.95, while new Easter hats were $5.00 and the holiday ensemble could be completed with a $1.69 handbag or $1.98 pair of gloves. The male of the species could be decked out for the Easter parade in a $16.95 spring suit for $2.00 down and ten weekly payments, accessorized with a $0.79 shirt, $0.21 socks and $0.38 necktie. Those who heeded Loveman's ad and made their way downtown the next day would certainly have something to tell their grandchildren about, but it would have nothing to do with those springtime bargains.

The big day of the week for shopping was well underway shortly after noon when assistant superintendent Albert Taylor noticed that yellowish-colored smoke was seeping into the street floor from somewhere underneath. Sales clerks and floorwalkers had been briefed as to how to react should this sort of emergency ever arise, and they calmly but firmly went through each floor and each department, herding customers and other employees outside in an orderly fashion. Incredible as it seems, contemporary reports indicate that four hundred Loveman's employees and approximately three hundred

This double-page spread appeared in the newspaper on Friday, March 9, 1934. The next day would definitely be a memorable one in Loveman's history, but not for the reasons given in this ad. *Author's collection.*

customers were evacuated in just over a minute. While this necessary procedure was going on, store electrician W.P. Reynolds and employee E.L. Owen found what they thought was the source of the fire and went to work with a portable fire extinguisher. This had little effect except to delay the notification of the fire department.

At 12:40 p.m., the belated call for help was made. A few weeks later, while the events of the day were still fresh in everyone's mind, Birmingham fire chief B.O. Hargrove set down in print his recollection of what he and his men found when arriving on the scene:

> *This particular fire was hard to handle, being in a building with an area of approximately 110 feet by 140 feet floor space where there was no basement, and with brick wall partitions ten feet apart under the first floor, extending the length of the building, where there was a basement. The walls of the building were brick, and the inner construction mostly rich pine and oil-soaked over a period of forty years or more. The fire was located under the first floor, gaining considerable headway along the 19th Street side of the building. The building had been burning a considerable length of time before the alarm was turned in, and at the time we arrived, practically twenty-five percent of the area was covered by a slow, smoldering fire and very hard to get at.*

As Chief Hargove's statement indicated, part of the initial problem in battling the fire was caused by the piecemeal fashion in which the Loveman's store had been constructed. The original 1891 structure facing Nineteenth Street had no basement, only a crawl space about four feet high, where many of the electrical cables were stuffed. One of those cables, either faulty or through being overloaded, was where the first spark had ignited. Obviously no firefighter's efforts could possibly be effective in a space barely tall enough to crawl through, so holes were chopped in the store's main floor in an attempt to reach a fire that had already spread beyond the area of its origin. "Men with hose lines went down and played a stream of water on the fire," Hargrove wrote. "Each man would stay until about to be overcome—in some cases were overcome—and another man would replace him." The larger section of the building, the part built in 1899, did have a basement that stretched along the Third Avenue side of the property. It was not being used as a "bargain basement"—Pizitz had gotten the drop on Loveman's with that concept—but it would have provided considerably more room for the firefighters' work had it been the source of the problem. Unfortunately, it was not.

While the firemen battled in cramped quarters inside, outdoors on the sidewalk, the customers and other spectators began to take stock of what had happened. There were many tales about incidents that had happened during the evacuation. One involved a lady who had been in the store's beauty salon, hooked up to a heavy floor-model hair curler. With everyone else having made a beeline for the outside, this stylish woman had no choice but to lift the big iron machine onto her shoulder and make her way out. Once on the sidewalk, she set the curler down to rest and then found she was unable to lift it again. In an incident that sounds like it came straight from a situation comedy script, it seems sheer fear had endowed her with temporary superhuman strength.

Another lady was trying on dresses in the ready-to-wear department when an employee pounded on the door and informed the clerk attending her that the building was on fire. The clerk and his customer did get out fast but not before the lady took time to pay for the dress she was wearing. Another employee left her area so quickly that she forgot her overcoat. Since it was a chilly day, she grabbed a sweater from a display table on the first floor, intending to return it afterward. Meanwhile, a customer named Mrs. Curl had obviously been paying attention to the newspaper ad the previous day and was in the store to buy a new Easter hat. When she reached the outside, she realized that she still had the hat on her head but had not paid for it. "I'll just send them a check," she decided. That hat and the borrowed sweater appear to have been the only two pieces of merchandise saved that Saturday afternoon.

Later, historian Jerry W. Laughlin recounted another incident that was amusing in hindsight:

While the spectators gathered outside and the firemen opened the floor inside, one employee was especially concerned about his hurried exit. He had left a cigar burning on a table and was afraid a serious fire might result. The man finally jumped the restraining ropes to race past police who tried to turn him back. Driven by his own sense of duty, he shouldered past them into the smoking store to retrieve his cigar. At least his area was safe...

Such major excitement was certain to catch the attention of local broadcast media, which of course at that time consisted solely of radio. WSGN personality Bill Cooper happened to be in the neighborhood with his literal "man-on-the-street" interview program known as *Inquiring Microphone*. His broadcast from 12:30 to 12:45 p.m. was originating from the sidewalk on Third Avenue North between Nineteenth and Twentieth Streets when his inquiring microphone picked up the sound of the first fire truck responding to the 12:40 alarm. As soon as his scheduled show ended, Cooper rushed to the scene and called the station to report that Loveman's was burning. WSGN engineers brought in extension wires, enabling Cooper to broadcast from the Blach's corner directly across from Loveman's. (Three years later, Blach's would move to the other end of the block to make way for the gleaming new S.H. Kress store on that corner—but I digress.) He was joined by the station's other staff announcers as the afternoon went on. Even future rural comedy superstar Pat Buttram was on hand, as he had a daily program on WSGN that highlighted his backwoodsy humor. As Loveman's smoldered, Buttram made his way through the crowd and cracked jokes from his usual small-town angle. It was shortly afterward that Buttram was added to the cast of the *National Barn Dance* on WLS in Chicago, and his legendary career in radio, movies and television began.

It was at about this point in the unfolding drama that the regular afternoon edition of the *Birmingham News* went to press with a headline that was to become a masterpiece of understatement: "Fire Damages Local Store." Subheadlines put a positive spin on the situation: "Flames at Loveman's Are Brought Under Control After Hour Fight—Business As Usual to Be Resumed at Once." The reporter elaborated:

With the blaze apparently under control, Joe H. Loveman, president, said it appeared the damage would be confined chiefly to smoke. Some damage was caused when firemen cut through the floor to reach the flames. Mr. Loveman said the store would be reopened during the afternoon if fire officials gave their approval. The store will be open Monday in any event.

Unknown to Loveman, the firefighters or anyone else, the fire had only been brought under control so far as they could see it. The Loveman's building, for whatever reason, had been constructed with an open space between its inner walls and the brick exterior, creating a draft. The fire that had supposedly been extinguished in the cramped subbasement was making insidious inroads up through this gap, basically surrounding the entire structure in an envelope of heated gas.

Finally, the envelope had been pushed as far as it could go, and around 3:00 p.m., things began to get ugly. About fifty firemen were still inside, believing they had put out the flames at their subterranean source, when Chief Hargrove encountered three of them running out of one of the doors on the Third Avenue side of the building. They informed him that they had heard fire crackling somewhere on either the second or third floor but they could not be certain which. Hargrove responded by ordering what was known as a "general alarm" and evacuating his men from the building—just in time, as it turned out.

Jerry Laughlin tells what happened next:

When the flames finally broke out, the store was like a huge matchbox waiting for a spark. The heated wooden floors burst into flames, rapidly leaping upward, bent on consuming the entire structure. Jagged tongues of flame poured out of every window. In ten incredible minutes the fire leapfrogged throughout the building, in faster time than anyone had ever seen any fire spread. A brisk northerly wind fanned the blaze and swirled smoke into the crowds of the curious.

Besides the naturally combustible nature of an 1890s building, Loveman's had another feature that helped seal its doom. On the balcony above the main floor, barrels of motor oil were stored for use in the automobile service department. Once the heat reached those barrels, they exploded and blew oil throughout the main floor, which certainly did not help any when it came to making the area flame retardant.

Shortly after that came proof positive it was the end of the road for the original Loveman's building. As described by witnesses, the iron and steel framework of the store's elevator system came crashing down, with a massive pinion gear landing on Third Avenue and cracking the windows in the Killgore Furniture Store across the street. Then it happened: smoke was pouring through the gaps between every brick in Loveman's façade, and the firefighters knew what that meant. They barely had time to clear out of the way before the walls fell ("roaring as if in agony," one spectator described it), bringing the roof down to basement level.

By this time, WAPI Radio had joined its competitor WSGN in broadcasting the tragedy. Engineer Idris Jones was carrying some eighty pounds of equipment with him along the sidewalk when a bystander shouted a warning to him. Looking up, Jones saw one of Loveman's walls falling directly toward him, and he later declared that despite his heavy load, he leaped three to four feet into the air in his haste to get across the street.

While Loveman's crumbled in on itself, the many stores and businesses in the surrounding blocks were affected in their own ways. Incredibly, some of them actually attempted to stay open for business even as it looked like Third Avenue was going to burn around them. Besides Killgore's, there were broken windows at the Vogue Shop, Duke Brothers Furniture, the Dan Cohen Shoe Store, Economy Shoe Mart and Roberts & Sons, all on the north side of Third Avenue, across the street from Loveman's. Woolworth's, at the time, was occupying a building on the northwest corner of Third and Nineteenth, and its five-and-ten-cent merchandise suffered damage from the debris of Loveman's crumbled walls.

The worst damage was on the other side of the Loveman's block, where the store was separated by an alley from Melancon's department store, Calder Furniture and Southern Bell's main telephone exchange offices. The Melancon's building was the former Louis Saks store that had replaced the Florence Hotel as Loveman's neighbor in 1916. By 1934, Melancon had subleased a portion of his building to the J.J. Newberry variety store chain. Newberry's fate would again intersect with that of the Loveman's building decades later—but that's a story for another chapter.

While the fire was underway, as luck would have it, Clem Melancon was on a business trip in New York City. Displaying a brand of loyalty unheard of in today's retail world, Lucille Long, the store's telephone operator, placed a long-distance call to Melancon, notifying him that his building was close to burning and asking his permission to close the store. Choking back smoke, Long remained at her switchboard until Melancon could call back and give the go-ahead to leave, upon which news Long fainted from smoke inhalation and had to be carried down five floors to the outside.

Much of Loveman's 1899 addition had crumbled by the time this photo was made, although the original 1891 portion of the building was still standing. At far left, notice the signage for Melancon's department store next door. *Birmingham Public Library Archives, Cat. #1556.12.73.*

Although Melancon's survived the fire, the Southern Bell offices were not nearly as fortunate. Shortly after Lucille Long got her awaited call from Clem Melancon, the fire made its way into the telephone exchange and effectively ceased most phone service in the downtown and southside parts of town. District manager R.E. Simmons reported that the long-distance board was a complete loss, and locally almost five thousand telephones were temporarily useless for anything but decoration. Emergency long-distance equipment was rushed from Atlanta and set up in the lobby of Southern Bell's office on Sixth Avenue, where absolutely necessary calls could be placed by showing up in person.

Now, what other major Birmingham landmarks adjoined Loveman's? Oh yes, there was the little matter of a showplace known as the Alabama Theatre. At the time the fire started, the Alabama was filled with youngsters on hand for the weekly meeting of the Mickey Mouse Club (a concept the enterprising Walt Disney would revive during the television era).

Understandably, there were many mothers shopping at Loveman's—and who were now standing around on the sidewalk—going into hysterics until their children could be located. In kind, there were a number of crying children in the crowd, evacuated from the movie palace and unable to locate their parents in the throng. All of that seemed to work out just fine in the end, though, and the concern became what was going to happen to the magnificent theater.

Separating the Alabama from the main part of Loveman's was the six-story all-steel Loveman's annex that had been constructed in 1917, some ten years

The Alabama Theatre almost became a victim of the same fire that consumed Loveman's but was saved by Loveman's "fireproof" annex and a thirty-six-inch firewall separating the two buildings. *Birmingham Public Library Archives, Cat. #1556.30.77.*

before the theater. When the Alabama was built next to the annex in 1927, some very far-seeing architect incorporated a thirty-six-inch-thick firewall separating the two structures. At some point, the firefighters thought to flood that firewall with water so the flames were not able to penetrate it. In addition, the roof of the Alabama was made of asbestos (which at that time was considered a good thing), so when sparks did fall onto it from next door, it remained intact.

At first, the broadcasters from WAPI thought the Alabama's roof would be a good vantage point for covering the fire, but it did not take long for them to decide they did not want to be quite that close to the story. They soon transferred operations to the upper floors and roof of the Pizitz store a block away. Meanwhile, down below, Louis Pizitz was demonstrating the philanthropy that had endeared him to Birmingham residents for the past thirty-five years. Even though there was no more fierce rivalry in the city's retail scene than that between Pizitz and Loveman's, now the time had come to temporarily set aside those feelings and tend to more important things. Louis Pizitz opened his store to serve as a sort of triage unit for firefighters who had been injured or overcome by the smoke and flames. For years afterward, those who were present at the scene recounted how the Pizitz sales counters were cleared of merchandise to be used as makeshift hospital beds, how Louis made his personal automobile available to transport the wounded and how he kept the firefighters supplied with refreshments. There would be plenty of time for the two department stores to get back to snarling at each other, but on this day, they were simply battling a common enemy together.

The fire department was finally able to declare the blaze "under control" (i.e., there was nothing left to burn) around 11:00 p.m. By that time, the temperature, which had been cold enough all day, had dropped to below freezing, and the water sprayed on what was left of Loveman's looked like it would have fit right in with the annual Christmas windows.

In the aftermath, the newspapers used page after page to recount every aspect of this most major turning point in downtown history. Proving that things were just as bad in 1934 as they are today when a disaster strikes, Birmingham's police chief flatly stated that anyone caught looting in the neighborhood around Loveman's would be shot to death on sight, no questions asked. The most amazing thing, often noted, was that despite the massive loss in property—generally estimated to be around $3 million—not a single life was lost among customers, employees or firefighters. That in itself was much to be thankful for.

After a much-needed day of rest on Sunday, everyone began trying to put their lives back together on Monday. The Alabama Theatre certainly had reason to yell and beat its chest, considering the way it had survived unscathed. In the place of its normal movie ad in the Monday newspaper, the Alabama instead printed this announcement:

> *WE ARE PROUD OF THE ALABAMA THEATRE—IT STOOD THE TEST! Unharmed by the mighty conflagration that demolished nearly a city block and came right to its doors, this fireproof, modern "Show Place of Birmingham" resisted the blaze. The theater remains intact, there is no damage to the contents of the building, the decoration or any of the marvelous furniture or fixtures.*
>
> *When the debris of the adjoining buildings has been cleared and the fire area opened again, we will resume operation. UNTIL THAT TIME, our entire personnel, our regular program of entertainment, our Alabama Theatre service will be temporarily installed at the TEMPLE THEATER.*

While there was not enough left of the Loveman's building to tell it had ever been there, the fact was that the annex did come through the fire still standing, at least. The interior was gutted, leaving charred office furniture and a partially missing roof, but that was more than remained of the main building. (The annex would be used for store offices for the next sixty years, but subsequent inspection in the 1990s revealed hidden areas of fire damage that had been untouched since 1934.) On that Monday afternoon, Loveman's officials made their way into the annex, where on the fourth floor was located the giant vault containing the store's official records and ledgers. To everyone's surprise, the contents were in perfect condition, credited to a group of firefighters who kept their hoses pouring water onto the vault's exterior for some two hours during the blaze.

The annex, however, was not going to be enough to get the store back on its feet. Joseph Loveman did not waste any time in securing a temporary home for his family's business, and his choice was a most logical one. A block away from

After the fire, Loveman's 1917 annex was the only part of the building still standing. Even it was severely damaged, as evidenced by this photo of the former store offices on the top floor, but it survived into the 1990s. *Birmingham Public Library Archives, Cat. #1556.26.20.*

the ruins, on the northwest corner of Third and Eighteenth, was a magnificent five-story structure that had opened in 1928 as the flagship of Birmingham's long-established Parisian department store, operated by the Holiner and Hess families. It was certainly neither of those families' fault that their huge building, meant to complement the Alabama Theatre, was only in business for a year before the stock market jumped out of an upper window on Wall Street and committed suicide. Parisian had been forced to downsize and move to smaller quarters on Second Avenue, so the 1928 building had been sitting vacant.

On Monday, March 12, Loveman's opened its temporary offices in the former Parisian building, and a few departments were even stocked with merchandise that had been stored in the company's warehouse at the time of the fire. (One has to wonder whether Joseph Loveman was recalling his promise to reporters that the store "would be open on Monday in any event" and did not want to make himself sound foolish.) The *Birmingham News* reported, "Resumption of full service to patrons awaits arrival of

This incredible angle, complete with handwritten notations, shows the complete destruction of the 1890s Loveman's structures. By this time, the store had already set up temporary headquarters a block away, in the former Parisian department store, awaiting the cleanup and construction of a new building. *Birmingham Public Library Archives, Cat. #1556.26.13.*

merchandise and fixtures…Meanwhile, preliminary plans are being speeded looking toward rebuilding on the site of the destroyed store."

It is indeed astonishing to see how quickly things were moving. The workmen set about their task of readying the former Parisian building with such a frenzy that one Loveman's executive cracked, "You'd think they were stockholders, they're so anxious for Loveman's to reopen as soon as possible." An opening date of March 28 was announced, and all efforts were concentrated toward making that deadline. The newspaper described the flurry of activity:

> *The third day after the fire, buyers were hurrying to New York to obtain new goods for Loveman's shelves. One of the railroads assigned a freight traffic expert to work with them to make speed between market and shelf. The new goods were stacked at Loveman's warehouse until the receiving and marking room in the basement of the temporary building was ready. Then a fleet of trucks began moving them.*
>
> *Meanwhile workmen had transformed the five floors. Greenish-blue walls glistened on the second floor where enameled shelves and counters were ready to hold silks and cottons and notions. Rosy walls with woodwork of cream and darker rose invited Easter finery to display itself on the third floor. Even while salespeople were sorting out goods yesterday afternoon, the last strips of beige carpeting were being unrolled for the top floors.*

Looking back on the events of March 1934, it seems particularly odd that in all the coverage, there was absolutely no mention of any reaction from City Stores to the total destruction of one of its primary holdings. Joseph Loveman was still running things, at least in a practical sense, and he was the official spokesman for the store during its transitional phase. He was quick to give credit to his capable staff for their hard work, though. "Everyone worked night and day, remodeling the store and getting everything in readiness for the opening," he told the *News*. Singled out for special mention was display manager Joe Apolinsky, who would still be occupying that position in the early 1970s. Due credit was also given to vice-president Paul Vaughan (later, half of the Vaughan-Weil partnership across the street).

And so, even as the Loveman's employees—none of whom, incidentally, lost a job due to the fire—settled in to what would be their home for the next year and a half, plans were being drawn up for a new building that would come to epitomize the Loveman's name for future generations. Soon, the memory of the old 1890s structures would be swept away like the burned rubble that had so recently taken their place.

Chapter 4

OUT OF THE ASHES

While Loveman's employees and customers adjusted to life a block away from the old homestead, as it were, the wheels of planning started to grind toward the eventual rebuilding. Everything was done quietly and without fanfare until Loveman's was ready to spring its plans on everyone, and that huge announcement occupied a goodly portion of the *Birmingham News*'s front page on August 21, 1934, just over five months after the same space had featured lurid photos of the fire.

The artists' rendering by the joint architectural firms of William E. Lehman of Cincinnati and Miller & Martin of Birmingham did indeed more closely resemble the structure that was eventually built than many other such preliminary plans. Apparently, most of the details had been worked out during the preceding months, leaving little or nothing to have to be improvised once construction began. In hindsight, one of the most important features of the August 1934 rendering was its inclusion of a clock on the store's corner, which had not been part of the old 1899 building. Instead of a vertical sign to replace the one the fire had crumpled, the Loveman, Joseph & Loeb name would be spelled out in subdued lettering across the two sides that faced Nineteenth Street and Third Avenue.

The article accompanying the architects' drawing spelled out in more detail just what sort of impressive edifice would soon rise from the vacant lot. Just as the destroyed building had been, the new Loveman's would encompass four floors, although with the addition of a "complete selling basement," as the reporter phrased it—no doubt the better to take business away from Pizitz's bargain basement, my dear. There would again be a mezzanine

A new, more elegant Loveman's rose from the ashes during 1935. *Rebecca Dobrinski collection.*

overlooking the first floor, and plans at that stage called for the roof to be "tiled and arranged for recreational and educational purposes and as a warehouse." Joseph Loveman was quoted as saying the new structure would have approximately 50 percent more selling space than the former building.

The exterior walls, perhaps in an effort to give it some continuity with the 1899 store's latter-day appearance, would be surfaced in Alabama limestone. Other than the almost-white coloration, though, the styles of the before-and-after buildings could hardly have been more different. We have already seen how the 1916 remodeling had stripped the old building of the remnants of its nineteenth-century ornamentation and reduced it to basically a huge box with windows. The 1934 plans clearly showed a building influenced by the current Art Deco craze. A later architectural historian compared the Loveman's appearance to that of being carved out of a single block of limestone.

All of these exterior elements were important, of course, but it was inside that the new Loveman's most dramatically parted ways with the old. "The entire building will be air conditioned both winter and summer," the newspaper gasped, "guaranteeing a comfortable temperature throughout the year."

Joseph Loveman's stated plan called for construction to begin that fall; however, unforeseen circumstances must have arisen, because it was not until late February 1935 that the contract for construction was awarded to

Cincinnati firm Frank Messer & Sons. By that time, the price for Loveman's new home was estimated to be around $1,200,000, living up to its promise to be "the largest and most impressive building erected here in the past 10 years." It would also be "one of the most modern department stores in the nation," and to prove the fact, one sentence mentioned that in addition to the air conditioning and six high-speed elevators, the new Loveman's would contain "moving stairways." Just what these mysterious inventions were was left to the reader's imagination for the time being.

On March 6, a date no doubt calculated to fall just short of a year since the fire, the ceremonial first shovel of dirt was turned to signal construction. Most of the work that immediately followed was carried out by dynamite rather than shovels, though, as the contractor burrowed deeper and deeper into the earth to reach the bedrock for the building's foundation. The newspapers faithfully followed the construction progress throughout that spring and summer, proudly pointing out that for the most part the new Loveman's was being built using Alabama materials and Alabama labor.

This photo was taken just prior to the opening of Loveman's new Art Deco–style building in November 1935. Notice that all the show windows are hidden by draperies, awaiting their grand unveiling. *Rebecca Dobrinski collection.*

Meet Me Under the Clock

It ended up taking just over eight months to complete this massive building program. A grand opening date of November 20 was announced, and in the days preceding, the Loveman's publicity machine shifted into overdrive to be sure the public was prepared for the wonders that awaited inside. The *Birmingham News* felt compelled to publish a congratulatory editorial on the occasion, which attempted to place the new Loveman's into a national perspective:

> *The significance of the enterprise is perhaps best illustrated by the fact that this is the first large department store building to be built in the United States in eight years. That the largest department store building to be erected anywhere in the country in that time should be built in Birmingham, and that it should have been started when we were still in the depths of the depression, after a devastating fire that might have given pause to the bravest and most optimistic of businessmen, are circumstances that make the achievement one to command the utmost attention.*

The day before the grand opening, article after article presented in incredible detail every possible facet of the new Loveman's. Thanks to that coverage, we know that the first floor contained the departments for gloves, handkerchiefs, hosiery, jewelry, linens, perfumes, cosmetics, candy, notions, silks, velvets, silverware, stationery, blouses, books, handbags, umbrellas, woolens, laces and trimmings, men's clothing, hats and shoes. That would be more than many smaller stores would feature throughout their entire structure, but Loveman's shoppers were only getting started.

The mezzanine had a beauty shop, lounge and tearoom and served as a preamble to the second floor, which Loveman's dubbed its "fashion floor." "It is hard to believe one is walking when one steps on the carpet with its thick pile, spread over approximately 3,000 square yards," the *News* solemnly stated. While floating through the luxurious carpet, shoppers on the second floor encountered gowns, furs, children's wear, hats, the girls' and juniors' departments, women's shoes, coats and housedresses. Care was taken to point out the expensive décor, including the gown room finished in English white sycamore and the millinery department with its period chairs and rare woods.

The third floor was given over to home furnishings, with what was considered a truly novel concept at the time. In the northwest corner of that floor was a replica cottage with six rooms and a foyer in which to display furniture as it would appear inside an actual home rather than out on a sales floor. This faux home contained a living room, dining room, breakfast room, nursery and two bedrooms, which was probably more than a lot of customers had in their own homes. (Nothing was mentioned about a replica bathroom with indoor plumbing, another luxury many people did not yet have at the time.)

The store's executive offices could be found on the fourth floor, sharing space with various housewares, glassware, china, kitchen cabinets, vacuum cleaners, radios, lamps, sewing machines, wallpaper and paint. For the new store's first month only, an extra attraction was added to these regular fourth-floor features. General Electric sent down the "Talking Kitchen" display that had recently been part of the 1933 Chicago World's Fair. As described by the *News*, the Talking Kitchen would come to electronic life, with the refrigerator, range and dishwasher engaging in witty conversation designed to point out all the most modern features of each. It may be no coincidence that this presentation sounds a lot like the famed Audio-Animatronic stage shows Walt Disney and his staff would amaze the public with almost thirty years later—in particular, Disney's Carousel of Progress, which happened to be General Electric's show at the 1964–65 World's Fair.

Now, what about that newfangled "moving stairway" that had been hinted at back in February? Apparently no one was yet familiar with the word "escalator," as the term was scrupulously avoided in the newspaper's description:

> *All you do is step right on, and without another motion on your part, you will be stepped right up from the first to the second floor in the new Loveman, Joseph & Loeb store. When you do this, you will be riding the first electric stairway to be installed in a store in Alabama.*
>
> *The electric stairway is located in the center rear of the main floor. It is finished in French walnut and aluminum, and is geared just the right speed—90 feet a minute—to carry one quickly and comfortably. Since it is the first installed in Birmingham, and since everyone will want to ride it, there will be an attendant on hand to guide those who may be a bit hesitant. Up it goes, and you will find another attendant to see that your first step-off is just right.*

We have already seen how Loveman's frequently tried to downplay its ownership by City Stores, but for the ceremonies around the grand opening, City Stores chairman of the board Albert Greenfield came down from Philadelphia and spared no words in conveying to the press just how strongly the company felt about its Birmingham branch. Besides a slew of other City Stores execs, also in town for the celebration were the presidents of the company's other outlets: Lit Brothers (Philadelphia), I. Ginsberg & Bros. (New York), Lowenstein's (Memphis), Maison Blanche (New Orleans) and Kaufman Straus (Louisville). Greenfield proudly announced that Loveman's was now not only the largest store in Alabama but in the entire South, "surpassing the Maison Blanche, one of the properties of City Stores I have just visited."

Those members of the general public who were lucky enough to join the City Stores dignitaries on opening day were presented with a souvenir brass key (which no doubt opened no actual lock within the building). These tiny artifacts still occasionally turn up in boxes or dresser drawers to this day.

Once all the opening festivities were over, the City Stores bigwigs went back to their respective branches and the Talking Kitchen moved on to wherever old World's Fair exhibits go. Loveman's then settled into its new life, and as the years went by, fewer and fewer people remembered that there had even been another building older than the present one. The construction of the new Loveman's did seem to spark a new interest in the development of the rest of its downtown intersection. In 1937, a gleaming new S.H. Kress variety store replaced the old Blach's building on the northeast corner of the Nineteenth Street/Third Avenue junction. In 1939, Woolworth's moved catty-cornered across from its old location to occupy a new structure on the southeast corner, a building modeled after the chain's flagship store in New York. That left only the northwest corner without a major retailer, and somewhat strangely, a progression of photos throughout the decades shows that nothing of any real consequence ever did operate there. Today, with the Loveman's, Kress and Woolworth buildings serving their later purposes well, the northwest corner is a parking lot.

Probably one of the rarest pieces of Loveman's memorabilia is this brass replica key that was given away to those who attended the grand opening of the new store. *Jerry Sklar collection.*

As I said earlier, one of Loveman's major contributions to that intersection was the clock on the corner. It followed the same Art Deco style as the rest of the edifice, with yellow hands against a black background, set into an octagon that somewhat resembled a sunburst. Before long, downtown shoppers began using the timepiece as a reference point, telling their companions to "meet me under the clock at Loveman's." Unlike the store's apparent earlier appropriation of the public's abbreviation of its name, all evidence seems to indicate that Loveman's never actually picked up the "meet me under the clock" saying for its own publicity purposes; it seems to have remained a colloquial saying among the populace rather than any sort of official advertising slogan.

(As a probably unrelated aside, perhaps it should be mentioned here that during the days when the giant iron statue of Vulcan was displayed at the Alabama State Fairgrounds, people had similarly instructed the other members of their entourage to "meet me at the feet of Vulcan." At just about the time Loveman's clock began ticking, Vulcan was being moved from the fairgrounds to his new, permanent home atop Red Mountain. Perhaps the people of Birmingham were simply always looking for a place to meet!)

Even more prominent than the clock were Loveman's twenty large display windows that lined both sides of the new building. As in the old one, keeping these windows constantly changing with new wonders to behold was the responsibility of Joe Apolinsky, and he took his job most seriously. His son Harold has related how, many times, he and his mother would be scheduled to meet Apolinsky for dinner after his day's work was done, but that family get-together time would be interrupted. "If Dad came out of the store, and walking along the sidewalk he noticed a single hatpin out of place on one of the mannequins, Mom and I would have to wait while he went back inside and fixed it, or it would have irritated him no end."

Since the new display windows were so much larger and more prominent than those that had been destroyed in the fire, they soon became miniature

For nearly fifty years, Loveman's display windows were the work of Joe Apolinsky. This Christmas greeting is a masterpiece of simplicity and understatement. *Harold Apolinsky collection.*

stages for all sorts of special events. In the spring of 1937, Loveman's decided to salute its own fiftieth anniversary (not counting its previous career in Greensboro) with what sounds like a most impressive series of tableaux illustrating Alabama's progress during those five decades. Huge oil paintings of steel mills, agriculture, a hydroelectric dam and other symbols of industry made up the backdrops for the scenes, with other objects—the raw materials used in making steel, for example—in the foreground. Complementing the theme, on the third floor was a museum of articles that were in use in Birmingham when Loveman's had first come to town.

The store's official golden anniversary date was decided upon as May 1, and much newsprint was taken up with articles comparing the status of things in 1887 as opposed to 1937. Joseph Loveman, in one interview, spelled out some of the major changes he had seen from his own perspective:

In the early days, one of the partners in the business went to Eastern markets twice a year, each time to buy a six months' supply of merchandise. Now the store has 94 departments and 43 buyers, each of them making from four to 15 trips a year to New York. Fifty years ago, a store bought for six months at a time and if some of the merchandise did not sell, it could be carried over into the next year. Today most merchandise is out of date within a few weeks.

Joe Apolinsky's Christmas windows for Loveman's also took on astounding depths of detail, as illustrated by this elaborate Nativity scene. *Harold Apolinsky collection.*

What of the next 50 years? We have faith that Birmingham will continue its phenomenal growth, and we hope that our own future will be as bright as our past.

By the way, remember in the last chapter that I said the stories of Loveman's and its neighbor Newberry's would be intersecting as we went along? Well, the next step in that direction took place in August 1936, when Clem Melancon announced that he was turning over his entire store building to the J.J. Newberry Company and leaving town. He took out a newspaper ad that read:

Saying good-bye to Birmingham and Alabama is indeed a hard thing to do, for this city and state has been very kind to me and my entire organization since my opening just three years ago. As the newspapers stated, I had a lease for ten more years, proving I had intended to make this city my future home. But the Newberry offer for the remaining ten years was so flattering, I was advised to accept it by the many civic leaders I consulted.

So now Loveman's had a new neighbor, and Clem Melancon moved to Daytona Beach, Florida, where he died in 1966. That isn't the end of the Loveman's/Newberry's association, though—you will just have to keep reading to find out how their histories eventually came to depend on each other. Suspenseful, isn't it?

An event that at one time might have generated much publicity in Birmingham, but that was treated as practically a footnote, was the death of Emil Loeb, the last surviving founder of Loveman's, at the age of seventy-seven on June 19, 1941. The fact that Loeb and his family had been living in New York since 1913 necessarily meant that his memory in Birmingham had somewhat faded, regardless of his name taking up a third of the space on the store's exterior signage. Loeb's passing was noted in the *Birmingham News* with only a couple of paragraphs totaling fewer than sixty words.

Emil Loeb's contribution to Birmingham retail history might have been almost forgotten in his former home city, but as of December 7, everyone's mind was on other things anyway. In hindsight, it is somewhat eerie to examine the ads that appeared in the newspaper that Sunday, giving no hint as to what was going to befall the United States before sunset. However, it is almost as strange to look at the papers in the days and weeks that followed. All the way through Christmas, Loveman's and the other Birmingham merchants continued to jingle their merry bells with absolutely no references to the escalating war against Japan and Germany. Perhaps this can be chalked up to the fact that the stores already had their Christmas advertising campaigns planned out ahead of time and it was easier to carry on as if nothing were wrong than to quickly rethink the whole procedure. Then again, perhaps the stores were merely subscribing to the same philosophy espoused by Winston Churchill in a radio address on Christmas Eve that year:

> *Here, in the midst of war, raging and roaring over all the lands and seas, sweeping nearer to our hearths and homes; here, amid all these tumults, we have tonight the peace of the spirit in each cottage home and in every generous heart. Therefore we may cast aside, for this night at least, the cares and dangers which beset us and make for the children an evening of happiness in a world of storm. Here then, for one night only, each home throughout the English-speaking world should be a brightly-lighted island of happiness and peace.*
>
> *Let the children have their night of fun and laughter, let the gifts of Father Christmas delight their play. Let us grown-ups share to the full in their unstinted pleasures before we turn again to the stern tasks and the formidable years that lie before us, resolved that by our sacrifice and daring these same children shall not be robbed of their inheritance or denied their right to live in a free and decent world.*

Indeed, poring over the gray pages of the *Birmingham News* on those rolls of microfilm, it does seem that the city wanted to wait until the holidays had passed before acknowledging the grim business of war. The front-page photo on January 1, 1942, depicted a smiling Baby New Year wearing a commando's helmet and gleefully manning a machine gun, showing that this was going to be a year unlike the past twenty or so. Still, the Loveman's ads made no direct reference to the war.

In fact, throughout the duration of the conflict, most of Loveman's treatment of it tended toward the "all together" spirit of ads, in which multiple downtown retailers jointly pledged their support for one cause or another, be it selling war bonds or encouraging housewives to save their excess grease.

While the war was going on, Loveman's acquired at least one new employee who would come to have a far-reaching effect in the future. Adele Chambordon (known affectionately as Del) went to work in Loveman's bookkeeping department around 1944, shortly after her high school graduation. At only four feet, two inches tall, it was admittedly difficult

During World War II, Loveman's did its part for the cause by giving over a portion of its usual window displays to promoting the common good, such as the sale of War Savings Bonds. *Birmingham-Jefferson History Museum collection.*

for Chambordon to be mistaken for any other employee. For almost forty years, Chambordon would be the chosen performer to ham it up whenever Loveman's needed such work; we will be examining her most famous role a couple of chapters from now.

There were occasional pauses in the unrelenting work of winning a war. When the Methodist church in Clay, Alabama, put out a request for help in purchasing a new bell to replace the original that had been stolen, Joseph Loveman came to the rescue. As one newspaper report phrased it, contacting a foundry in Baltimore did no good because "guns and tanks and bombs are made for wars, and not church bells." The bell Loveman finally purchased for the church had formerly belonged to the Black Diamond Coal Mining Co. of West Blocton.

When it appeared the war might tentatively be drawing to a close, it seemed everyone was ready for any sort of news about the brave new postwar world. In early May 1945, three months before the official end of the conflict, Loveman's sprang on the public its plans for the immediate

The rich woodwork and interior design of Loveman's main floor can be savored in this 1940s view of the cosmetics counter. *Rebecca Dobrinski collection.*

future. As happened so often during that transitional period in United States history, some of the plans eventually materialized while others did not. Among the most interesting in the latter category was a much-hyped goal of adding two floors to the top of Loveman's already four-story structure. Photos sent to the *Birmingham News* included dotted lines to show just how the two extra floors would appear.

The other expansion plan might have seemed more practical, but it, too, would have its own delayed advent. Loveman's had bought the five-story McKelvey-Coats Furniture building that fronted Second Avenue and announced its intention to turn the old store into a completely modern "store for the home," to be connected with the main building by a bridge over the alley separating the two. Although Loveman's planned to spend $850,000 on the projects of adding floors and creating the new home furnishings store, it was announced that McKelvey-Coats had not yet made arrangements to vacate its building, so that part of the scheme would have to wait.

And so they waited…and waited…as 1945 turned into 1946, and 1946 turned into 1947, with no apparent progress in either of the grand schemes.

Loveman's always seemed to be on the cutting edge when it came to celebrity-related promotions. This display highlights the girls' clothing endorsed by child superstar Margaret O'Brien. *Birmingham-Jefferson History Museum collection.*

Part of the delay might be chalked up to the fact that Joseph Loveman's health was failing. On the front cover of the store newsletter for December 1946, he wrote to his employees: "Once again in the spirit of the Christmas season, I want to wish to each of you the best of God's blessings now and in the year ahead. May you know the realization of your heart's desire and may peace and good will abide among you."

It would be his final holiday season as president of the store bearing his family name. During 1947, former executive vice-president O.W. Schanbacher was promoted to president of Loveman, Joseph & Loeb, while Joseph Loveman was elevated to the figurehead position of chairman of the board. This removed Loveman from the stress of the day-to-day operations while still allowing him to be around as often as he felt like doing so.

Fortunately, the veteran merchant was in fine form on June 20, 1949, when the new Store for the Home had its grand opening (a little over four years after it had been announced). Loveman cut the ceremonial ribbon after receiving a standing ovation from the crowd, and a reported twenty-three thousand customers were on hand to examine the new addition. Just to be sure the remodeled McKelvey-Coats building matched the rest of Loveman's, architects' chores were turned over to Miller, Martin & Lewis, the same Birmingham firm that had been involved with the 1935 construction program.

The newspaper described the upscale departments that could be found in the new Store for the Home:

> *On the first floor are crystal and chinaware, arranged in racks lighted from beneath. Floor coverings are displayed on the second floor. The third features draperies, a china shop and the interior decorating department.*

In June 1949, Loveman's opened its much-anticipated Store for the Home in what had formerly been the McKelvey-Coats furniture store fronting on Second Avenue North. *Jerry Sklar collection.*

53

Living room furniture, pictures and mirrors are on the fourth floor, while the top floor is given over to bedroom and dining room furniture. The entire annex is lighted throughout by recessed ceiling lights and bullet spotlights.

There was one important word buried in that description: "annex." Yes, even though the 1917 annex fronting Third Avenue and separating Loveman's from the Alabama Theatre had been renovated after the fire and used for store offices, for most employees from the late 1940s on, when one spoke of the "annex," one meant the Store for the Home building. It definitely was a true annex, completely separate from the main store but connected by those planned "enclosed bridges" on the second, third and fourth floors.

Christmas had always been the biggest time of the year in the retail world, but with the United States' unprecedented postwar prosperity, the holiday season became even bigger and brighter. Loveman's piled the gifts high on the sleigh for the 1949 Christmas season, filling a full-page newspaper ad

Those who grew up in the 1950s can still recall the magic of visiting the huge downtown department stores during the Christmas season. It looks like Joe Apolinsky and his crew of merry elves had been working overtime to deck the halls for this photo. *Harold Apolinsky collection.*

with sixteen paragraphs, each describing a different feature the store was offering. The street floor was adorned with "lovely blue and white Christmas decorations," and one of the display windows facing Nineteenth Street was devoted to an animated interpretation of the life of Santa Claus. The jolly old gent could be found in person on the fourth floor, taking time out at 4:30 p.m. each day to broadcast over WAPI Radio. Just in case any kids were nervous about sitting on St. Nick's furry lap, a mailbox was provided under the clock on the corner, and youngsters were encouraged to drop their letters in for a special delivery service to the North Pole.

But that was only the beginning. "Toyland" all but took over the third floor, presided over not by Santa but by local Birmingham clown Bobby Bumps. An enormous electric train display made boys (and their dads) drool with anticipation as it chugged its way through a succession of miniature scenes. The third floor also housed a Western Corral, with the latest toys and duds, and a Doll House for those who wanted something more cuddly than a pair of spurs.

Finally, based out of the main floor were "Santa's Christmas Belles," described thus: "A group of ambitious young ladies in holly-berry red jackets are waiting to serve you in any possible way. They'll make gift suggestions, answer questions, give you valuable information and assistance concerning Loveman's!"

But as Al Jolson might have said, "You ain't seen nothin' yet!" The 1950 Christmas season was going to be even bigger and brighter—and for all those people who like to grumble that when they were kids stores did not begin promoting Christmas until after Thanksgiving, let the record show that Santa moved into Loveman's third floor lock, stock and reindeer on November 11 that year.

Loveman's had a new holiday character to promote for 1950, though, in addition to the bearded guy in the red suit. Down at City Stores' New Orleans outlet, Maison Blanche, the 1948 Christmas season had seen the introduction of Mr. Bingle, a diminutive marionette snowman who had wings made of holly leaves and wore an inverted ice cream cone for a hat. (It was no coincidence that Maison Blanche and Mr. Bingle also shared the same set of initials.) A Bingle TV program in New Orleans had proven so successful in 1949 that in 1950, the happy holiday helper was recruited to bring his particular brand of magic to Loveman's.

Obviously no one in Birmingham would have known who Bingle was unless they were a recent transplant from New Orleans, but that did not prevent Loveman's—no doubt with the behind-the-scenes encouragement

The crew from Dixie Neon installed the giant Mr. Bingle decoration above Loveman's corner clock for the second year in 1951. *Dixie Neon collection.*

of City Stores—from treating his arrival as if he were a major celebrity. On the store's exterior corner, just above the clock, a three-story effigy of Bingle loomed over the sidewalk below, with a sign bearing that year's slogan: "Mr. Bingle is here with Christmas cheer!" Bingle was the new star of the animated window displays, and Loveman's also took full advantage of the emerging power of television by sponsoring a daily Bingle TV show on WAFM, Channel 13. The program was actually broadcast live direct from a special puppet stage on Loveman's third floor; getting his first TV experience as the puppeteer and voice of Mr. Bingle was a future Birmingham television legend, Cliff Holman, later known by young and old as "Cousin Cliff."

Actually, Holman and his new bride, the former Ann Kyle, had been around Loveman's for a while, each toiling anonymously among the store's hundreds of other employees. Holman worked in the credit department, and he enjoyed telling the story of one of his more unusual responsibilities in that capacity. It seems that Loveman's sold refrigerators that came equipped with what sounds like a rather odd feature: an attached meter, into which a

Wondering how the departments were laid out on Loveman's third floor in 1950? This handy newspaper ad gives all the answers. This was before a hole was cut into the center of the floor to make room for escalators in 1955. *Author's collection.*

specified number of coins had to be placed in order to keep the motor running. The accumulated cash could subsequently be applied toward purchasing the refrigerator. The future Cousin Cliff found himself being sent out to homes throughout the Birmingham area with the job of collecting the coins from the meters. Human nature being an old, established tradition, Holman said that he found homeowners who had devised the most ingenious ways of bypassing the meter and keeping their refrigerators operating without having deposited the requisite money. This inherent flaw probably explains why you aren't having to keep quarters, dimes and nickels on hand in your kitchen to keep your frozens from spoiling today.

At the other end of the economic spectrum, Loveman's snagged the lucrative and prestigious honor of outfitting each year's Miss Alabama for her big journey to Atlantic City for the Miss America contest. Led by longtime fashion coordinator Ninette Griffiths, this paid off in a big way when Yolande Betbeze, Miss Alabama of 1950, was chosen as Miss America for 1951. Her ascension to power was a point of pride for the whole state, but Loveman's especially used the turn of events to its advantage.

Ms. Betbeze had barely begun her yearlong reign when the Loveman's world was shaken by the news that most of its employees knew was inevitable: Joseph Loveman died at 2:30 a.m. on February 28, 1951, at his home at 2842 Hastings Road (having earlier moved out of his original home on

Miss Alabama is gowned by Loveman's to compete for the

Miss America title

So that our new queen of beauty will enter the national competition in Atlantic City with all of the assistance we can possibly offer, Loveman's presents Miss Alabama with her entire contest wardrobe, and puts at her disposal our fashion shops, fashion staff and beauty salon.

Miss Alabama not only selects clothes from our extensive collections in the fashion shops and Designers' Room but is given especially planned and purchased creations from world-famous couturiers so her wardrobe can be custom-designed to enhance her own loveliness and individuality.

According to a consensus of writers who have witnessed the judging for many years our own Miss Alabama is always one of the best-dressed contestants in the pageant. We are proud and happy that we can contribute to this distinction.

LOVEMAN'S

For decades, Loveman's and its fashion coordinator, Ninette Griffiths, were responsible for dressing the young ladies who bore the title of Miss Alabama at the annual Miss America contest in Atlantic City. *John Lehman collection.*

Rhodes Circle). He was sixty-nine years old and confined to a wheelchair; however, he had made his final visit to the store the day before his death. His multiple obituaries that ran in the newspapers over the next few days did a magnificent job of recapitulating his long career, although, staying true to form, they still gave no hint that he was A.B.'s adopted, rather than biological, son.

There was also some mention that Loveman had been a member of Birmingham's original housing authority from 1940 until 1949. That explains the existence to this day of a government housing project known as Loveman Village, which was established in 1952. Unfortunately for the memory of Joseph Loveman and the goals he pursued during his time with the housing authority, Loveman Village (at least as of this writing) is today known only for its notoriously high crime and poverty rates.

Loveman's funeral was held on March 1, and he was buried in Elmwood Cemetery. The *Birmingham News*, in an editorial that day, tried to sum up how many Birmingham citizens felt about the departed chairman of the board, while employees of the store contributed their memories of their late boss. His multiple secretaries went on record as saying one of his greatest joys was making anonymous contributions wherever he saw a need. "Many young persons owe their educations to him," they said. "In some instances even the ones he helped didn't know who their benefactor had been. He didn't like to be thanked and he didn't want publicity."

Unlike the Pizitz store, which remained in the hands of Louis Pizitz's descendants even after the death of their patriarch, the passing of Joseph Loveman meant the end of any involvement by the descendants of the original founders. His only son, A.B. (named in honor of his grandfather), was serving as a doctor in Louisville, Kentucky, at the time of Loveman's death. His three daughters—Mrs. Lewis Hirsch of Louisville and Mrs. M.D. Blumenthal and Mrs. J.H. Oppenheimer of Birmingham—produced a number of grandchildren for Loveman, but none of them chose to be involved in the management of the store. For the first time since 1870, Loveman, Joseph & Loeb was not being operated by anyone named Loveman, Joseph or Loeb.

Chapter 5

IT'S NICE TO HAVE YOU
IN BIRMINGHAM—MAYBE

E ven though Joseph Loveman's absence would certainly be noticed throughout the company, the fact that he had retired from active duty a few years before meant that he would be missed more philosophically than practically. One major change that came about some time in the months surrounding his death epitomized some of the "moving ahead" philosophy of the times.

Although the abbreviated Loveman's name and logo had been appearing in ads for years, and who knows how many years of popular usage preceded that, the signage on the Third Avenue and Nineteenth Street sides of the building still spelled out its full, official name of Loveman, Joseph & Loeb. With the last of the three now gone, those letters were removed and replaced with a much larger logo reading simply LOVEMAN'S. Although the new signage was created by Birmingham's now-legendary Dixie Neon company, befitting the store's upscale image, these were not flashing, gaudy neon spectaculars. Each separate letter in Loveman's was made of dark green metal, and each was individually backlit in white at night. The overall effect was to produce a dark letter with a sort of halo-like glow surrounding it. After the replacement signage was in place, pretty much the only reminder of the store's full name was in the entrance bays, which still bore miniature coats of arms with the three intertwined letters LJL.

In other ways, the store clutched its history to its chest as if it were Linus Van Pelt's security blanket. But preserving the past had to go hand in hand with taking advantage of more modern developments. That one-eyed living room invader known as television had made its way into Birmingham during the summer of

Perhaps unintentionally, the photographer caught two different styles of the Loveman's logo in this single shot: the new signage on the building and the "script" lettering on the ad on the bus parked in front. *Rebecca Dobrinski collection.*

1949. Pizitz sank quite a bit of its advertising budget into the new medium, but evidence is scarce as to just how deeply Loveman's joined it. It is known that by November 1952, Loveman's was the sponsor for the presidential election night coverage on WBRC-TV (then Channel 4, soon to become Channel 6). Actually, we should say that Loveman's shared sponsor duties with the Philco company, in the hope of getting more people to buy those newfangled TV sets at the department store. (They had recently begun taking up space on the fourth floor that had formerly been devoted to other merchandise.) Eisenhower might have been the winner of the big election, but Loveman's and Philco were right up there on the platform as his running mates—at least in Birmingham.

That Christmas, the entire building was decked out as usual, but by this point, Mr. Bingle was beginning to melt into the background. The corner decoration that year, erected by the hardy Dixie Neon crew, was a two-story Santa Claus emerging from an icicle-draped chimney. Bingle, reduced to a mere fraction of his former outdoor decoration size, perched on the rim of the chimney, barely noticeable. The interior decorations still featured the two holiday harbingers equally, with the earlier slogan modified to "We are here with Christmas cheer."

Although Mr. Bingle was a vital part of City Stores' Christmas advertising well into the 1970s, he only appeared at Loveman's in the early 1950s. Here, he is relegated to a supporting role on the sign in this window loaded with perfect Yuletide gifts. *Birmingham-Jefferson History Museum collection.*

A rather old-fashioned-sounding concept in these days of huge retailers that stay open twenty-four hours a day, seven days a week is the announcement that appeared in the newspapers on the first day of 1953. At that time, normal business hours for Loveman's were 10:00 a.m. to 5:30 p.m. Anyone who could not shop earlier or later than that was out of luck. However, that sprawling retailer down the block, Sears, set a precedent by staying open later on Monday and Friday nights. Loveman's finally decided to give it a try and began staying open until 8:30 p.m. on Mondays. What about those employees who were already working a full shift every day? Don't worry about them; on the days the store stayed open until that late hour, Loveman's would not open until noon. Truly, shopping was done at a more leisurely pace in those long-ago days.

Lazy days had to take a temporary vitamin shot whenever a big store event was planned. One of the biggest was in the fall of 1953, when former silent movie superstar Gloria Swanson made a personal appearance at Loveman's to promote her line of "Forever Young" dresses. Swanson was no longer so forever

Loveman's had a star in its eyes once again when silent film star Gloria Swanson went into the ladies' fashion business in 1953. *Birmingham-Jefferson History Museum collection.*

young herself by that time, but the store spared no effort to welcome her and let everyone know she was going to be there. Stars from the music world also dropped by Loveman's "record bar" on the fourth floor whenever there was an opportunity for them to promote and autograph their latest releases.

Throughout all these highly promoted events, the rivalry between Loveman's and Pizitz simmered and stewed. With the two buildings only a block away from each other, the competition was quite naturally concentrated in a relatively small area. (It was a good thing the J.J. Newberry building stood between them, something like the referee in a prizefight.) Their constant attempts at oneupmanship were tempered with reason. For example, no Loveman's employee would be fired for taking his or her children to see Pizitz's annual window displays at Christmas. But for all the good-natured ribbing that went on, underneath, the competition was very real and very serious.

Del Chambordon recalled one example that would produce most uncomfortable results: if Pizitz began promoting some brand-new item that Loveman's did not have. As she tells it, the buyer for that particular department would be called in by upper management and given the third degree as to why they had let Pizitz get the upper hand. Such occurrences in any department were necessarily rare or else that buyer would likely be looking for a new job.

While all of this was at its peak, on April 19, 1953, Loveman's fired the first volley in a campaign that was sure to kick the contest up several notches. It became the first of the two businesses to announce it would open—gasp!—a branch store. Pizitz had long boasted in its advertising that the reason it was so dependable was that it had one store, and one store only, to be concerned about. We have already seen that after the City Stores purchase in the mid-1920s, Loveman's had gone out of its way to downplay the effects of being part of a "chain." Branch stores were another matter, and Loveman's bragged that it was going to build the first Birmingham department store branch outside Jefferson County. A huge new shopping development was in the planning stages in what was then the new, exciting neighborhood known as Normandale, on the south side of Alabama's capital city, Montgomery. The Montgomery architectural firm of Sherlock, Smith and Adams unveiled its rendering of a new two-story Loveman's to be the centerpiece of the new Normandale shopping center. The article accompanying the architects' concept art specified that the Normandale branch would contain 100,000 square feet, of which 80,000 would be devoted to retail.

While work progressed apace at Normandale, Loveman's lobbed another one at Pizitz closer to home. On March 29, 1954, a new Loveman's branch opened in what had formerly been the venerable Erlick's department store at 1916 Second Avenue in downtown Bessemer. The next day, the newspaper reported on the enthusiasm that greeted Loveman's arrival in its new home:

> Several hundred persons gathered in front of the new department store more than an hour in advance of tape-cutting ceremonies and a welcome by Bessemer mayor Jap Bryant. Following the opening ceremonies, crowds flocked into the store.
>
> The new store, which occupies a two-story building, is fully air-conditioned and contains 20,000 square feet of floor space. Remodeling and equipping the store cost approximately $250,000.
>
> Loveman president O. W. Schanbacher said, "This is an eventful day in the history of Loveman's. We feel this store will be an asset to Bessemer, and hope to grow as Bessemer grows."

One endorsement came from Julian Erlick, whose own store had formerly occupied the building. He told the press the new store

In 1954, Loveman's opened its first branch in the former Erlick's department store on Second Avenue in downtown Bessemer. *Jerry Sklar collection.*

"incorporates every shopping convenience, and would be a credit to a city of a million people." The manager of the new Bessemer branch was Harry Cohn, who would soon be moving down to Montgomery to help things move normally in Normandale.

Yes, it took a year and a half to get it done, but the Normandale shopping center (complete with Loveman's) had its grand opening on September 10, 1954. Obviously, people in Montgomery were not nearly as familiar with the Loveman's story as those who had lived through most of it in Birmingham, so that city's newspapers ran numerous features explaining the new store's origins. Even more space was devoted to the wonders of the newest branch of the company, with one article explaining just how the Normandale outlet was arranged:

> *The first and second floors are connected by the first electric stairways to be installed in Montgomery. First floor departments include a ready-to-wear division, children's department from layette to pre-teens, boys' and men's clothing and furnishings, accessories and a complete shoe department for the entire family.*
>
> *On the second floor, which may also be reached by elevator, is a complete home furnishings store, with full assortments of everything from curtains*

The second Loveman's branch store to open was the centerpiece of Montgomery's Normandale shopping center in September 1954. *Dixie Neon collection.*

to TV, from glassware and gifts to floor coverings and refrigerators. Also on the second floor are piece goods and patterns, a sporting goods department and a toy department.

Loveman's officials seemingly spared no expense when it came to making sure the exterior of their Normandale store was as impressive in its own way as the gleaming Art Deco flagship store in Birmingham, taking into account the changing tastes in architecture since 1935. The front of the first floor was surfaced with reddish-brown marble brought from Colorado. "All this marble was cut from a single piece, and has been so placed that veins run matched through continuously with almost invisible joints," the Montgomery paper reported. If anything, the exterior of the second floor was even more impressive. It was surfaced with Roman travertine marble from Italy, its wide expanse broken only by the Loveman's signage (the same style as the green metal letters in Birmingham). More marble chips were used on the inside, where the ground level's terrazzo floor was sprinkled with embedded black marble speckles.

The building's most noticeable features were the two huge display windows on either side of the upper level. These could be used for any number of changing displays, but those who grew up in Montgomery particularly remember the transformation that took place each Christmas. One of the two windows became the Normandale outlet for that jolly old elf from the

Many native Montgomerians fondly remember the Normandale Loveman's giant window in which jolly old St. Nick would hold audience with his young admirers while the public watched from below. *David Robertson collection; photo by Paul Robertson Sr.*

North Pole, and it became a cherished Montgomery tradition to sit in the parking lot and watch the youngsters having their audience with St. Nick. When Normandale and Loveman's began an additional custom of erecting a huge Christmas tree in the parking lot directly in front of the store, the Yuletide tableau was even more appealing.

As exciting and new as the new Normandale branch was, that did not mean things were being neglected back on the home range in downtown Birmingham. In fact, the enthusiasm generated by the happenings in Montgomery seems to have reenergized the main store like a jolt of electricity. And speaking of electricity, you may recall that one of the novelties of the 1935 Loveman's building was the first "electric stairway," aka escalator, ever seen in Birmingham. As you just read, the Loveman's at Normandale introduced the first escalator to be seen in that city too. However, at the flagship store, the escalator still connected only the first and second floors, with all other shopping areas accessed by elevators.

In 1947, Pizitz had taken the bold step of installing its first escalators all the way from the street floor to the fourth floor and wasted no effort in boasting of that fact. Loveman's belatedly got the picture and, in September

Loveman's had had an escalator—the first in Birmingham—between the first and second floors since its 1935 construction, but at the time of this 1955 view, that area was blocked off so the escalators could be extended all the way from the basement to the fourth floor. *Author's collection.*

1955, put its "seven new moving stairways," as the newspaper called them, into operation:

> *Costing approximately $250,000, the new moving stairways provide escalator service from the basement to the fourth floor, going both up and down. The moving stairway that moves down from the second to the first floor will carry 8,000 persons an hour. All other moving stairways in the store will each transport 5,000 persons hourly.*

Store manager Robert Jenista made the revelation that when the 1935 construction was underway, provision had been made in the framing of the building so additional escalators could eventually be added. "The people who planned the building showed great foresight," he told the press. "This enabled us to do the job faster and at a greatly reduced cost."

Another spiffy new improvement made during this period was seen by even more people than the seven escalators. With absolutely no advance warning and no explanation given, readers who opened their newspapers on the morning of Sunday, February 12, 1956, suddenly saw a brand-new Loveman's logo topping the ads. For most of the 1950s, the Loveman's logo had simply consisted of the name in a script font. Prior to that, it tended to change from ad to ad, sometimes in a decorative typeface but at other times set in plain block type. The 1956 logo, which would endure for the rest of the store's life, incorporated elements of both. The "LOVEMAN'S" name, in all uppercase letters, appeared in a serif font that looked rather squashed—that is, the letters were wider than they were tall. The most distinctive part, though, was a huge, graceful "L" made of sweeping lines and curlicues that overlapped the first couple of letters. The "L" would, in effect, become Loveman's monogram, frequently appearing in places where the full word might have been cramped. As some of the photographs in this book will attest, it also became the most difficult part of the logo to duplicate, particularly by sign painters, who could never seem to get the proportions to match the way it looked in printed form.

It would seem the adaptation of the new logo might have been a rather sudden decision on Loveman's part, as the signage on the downtown, Bessemer and Montgomery stores continued to reflect the earlier style. In fact, none of those branches would ever have exterior signage matching the new logo, although it would be re-created for branches that would be opening in the future. It was also around this same time—perhaps even simultaneously— that the store's official name was changed from Loveman, Joseph & Loeb to Loveman's of Alabama. A big part of the reason for this move was that, as marketing and media continued to expand, the Birmingham Loveman's was finding itself more and more often confused with the other stores of that name, particularly Loveman's of Chattanooga. There were times the two completely separate Loveman's found themselves being dunned for the other's unpaid bills simply because the invoices in question had been made out to the wrong one.

As the annual store anniversary sale rolled around again in the spring of 1957, Loveman's (of Alabama, you understand) was able to celebrate 70 years of business in Birmingham. A newspaper ad proudly illustrated the fifty-four current Loveman's employees who had been with the firm for 25 years or more, for a combined total of 1,705 years. The real old-timers each had 37 years of service under their nametags: Elizabeth Brown, Bessie Walker, Martin Coker and, yes, Joe Apolinsky, whose fine display work showed no sign of slowing down (and he still had approximately 13 more years to go!). The others ranged downward from 36 to 25 years and included quite a few African American employees—a fact one might need to bear in mind as we draw toward the close of this chapter.

By the 1958 Yuletide season, Loveman's had come up with a new annual slogan that would be used for years to come: "The Christmas Tree Store." To help make the point, the building's corner over the clock—where Santa and Mr. Bingle had originally towered over shoppers—was bedecked with a Christmas tree several stories tall. Fittingly for Loveman's upscale image, the tree was dark green and decorated with golden pears and ornaments; during the 1960s, Pizitz would debut its own corner tree, fashioned from neon-green tinsel and bearing huge fluorescent red candles. Strangely, of the many preserved photos showing Loveman's Christmas decorations, none seems to have survived that include the corner tree.

Advertising, of course, was a year-round job for the Loveman's staff, hardly confined to the Christmas season. In the spring of 1959, executives were crowing about winning a "gold award" from the National Retail Merchants Association in recognition of the previous four years of the store's newspaper ads. O.W. Schanbacher presented the award to director of advertising William Spoor, who in turn gave much of the credit to layout artist Winifred Karger and copywriter Helen Hilley. One point that seemed well worth bragging about is that Loveman's won the award by beating out legendary retailer Neiman-Marcus and its ads in the *Dallas Morning News*.

There was certainly never any downtime for the advertising department, as each month brought new elements to promote. Sometimes it was an improvement in the store building, such as in October 1959 when the new "V.I.P. Shop" opened as an adjunct to the traditional Store for Men. Other ad campaigns were built around that springtime tradition known as AEA (Alabama Education Association) Week, when schoolteachers from every part of the state gathered in Birmingham for five days of meetings. All of the downtown department stores polished up their shiniest apples for the teachers. No matter what the season, the busy elves in the advertising department managed to turn out one eye-popping creation after another.

Now, if this story were being told in a documentary instead of a book, this is the point at which the background music would start to change from a happy tune to ominous tones. Things had been going so well for Loveman's—ever since the recovery from the fire, in fact—that trouble was sure to muscle its way into the act sooner or later. The store was about to enter the three most trying years it would ever face, so as Bette Davis might have said, fasten your seat belts…it's about to be a bumpy ride.

The V.I.P. Shop for men took up space underneath the main-floor mezzanine beginning in 1959. *Author's collection.*

Perhaps in hindsight, it could have been taken as a premonition when the first blow fell. On September 17, 1960, store president O.W. Schanbacher, the immediate successor to Joseph Loveman, suddenly died of a heart attack at age fifty-eight. His demise was more than unexpected; a store employee was driving him home when the attack hit him, and he was pronounced dead on arrival at University Hospital.

Schanbacher's obituaries, as usual, enumerated his many charitable efforts and the civic organizations to which he belonged. The true measure of his character, though, was the way the Loveman's employees felt about him. To hear their reminiscences over the succeeding years, it would seem that Birmingham never had a more consistently beloved boss than O.W.

Schanbacher—unless it was the equally sainted Roper Dial of Sears, and reports are that Dial and Schanbacher were such close friends that they could often be found strolling together along the downtown streets. So distressing was Schanbacher's death that Loveman's closed for the entire day of his funeral, and as we have seen, that sort of tribute was reserved for only the most significant individuals indeed.

Schanbacher's immediate successor as store president was Paul L. Dowd, a fifty-two-year-old Harvard graduate who had joined Loveman's as executive vice-president and general merchandise manager in 1959, so his ascension to the position of president in early May 1961 was not exactly like bringing in a stranger. Before his tenure was over, though, he might have felt like a stranger in a strange land, because he was to face challenges that no other Loveman's president had ever had to deal with.

While Loveman's was getting settled into the idea of a new president, there was a bit of activity next door at the J.J. Newberry building. Remember that I have told you repeatedly—and will be saying again—that the stories of these two businesses are eventually going to overlap, but for now you'll just have to be patient. The big news for Newberry's in May 1961 was that it had expanded from a traditional five-and-ten (or, more correctly, variety) store into a full-blown department store. Now, in addition to trinkets and inexpensive toys, Newberry's also had a three-hundred-seat luncheonette and cafeteria, a men's clothing department, furniture departments and other such features that brought it closer to what its bookend neighbors, Loveman's and Pizitz, were doing. This remodeling program is also what gave Newberry's the distinctive blue-green metal facing (the company's logo color) that would cover much of the 1916 building's architecture.

So after all that effort, it remains a mystery to this day why, a year and a half later, in December 1962, the Newberry's signage was suddenly removed and a new logo, Britt's, was erected in its place. The news coverage treated the switch as if it were the advent of a brand-new department store, but the exact origin of Britt's was left somewhat hazy: "Britts of Birmingham is one of a group of department stores, scheduled to number 53 in the next two years, that maintain a buying office at 245 Fifth Avenue in New York City." However, if one closely examines the yellowed newspaper clippings, the fact jumps out that the same company president, John E. Nelson of New York, presided over both the Newberry's remodeling and the Britt's grand opening, showing that the two were different heads off the same body, as it were. Due to this timing, it would be Britt's and not Newberry's that would be making news in the coming year.

Loveman's barely acknowledged the aqua-colored antics going on in the other half of its block, because 1962 was to be celebrated as its seventy-fifth anniversary year. With a slogan of "The best to you in '62," Loveman's sent out the following preview:

> *When a business reaches its 75th anniversary year, there is a temptation to look back sentimentally on the past—to reminisce. But Loveman's believes this is an auspicious occasion to move enthusiastically into the years ahead.*
>
> *Beginning at once, Loveman's is launching into a complete renovation of its Third and Fourth floors in the main store. All office spaces are being moved from these two floors into our Second Avenue building, on the upper floors.*
>
> *The entire area in the main store building on the Third and Fourth floors is being completely redesigned and decorated to provide first-class departments.*
>
> *Additional floor space is being built between our building and the Alabama Theatre building to provide greater stock areas on the Third and Fourth floors. It's a big job of major moving and construction. We hope you will be patient with our disorder during the next many weeks.*

Disorder was indeed going to be the name of the game, but not only for the reasons Loveman's expected. As most people know, by late 1962 and early 1963, Birmingham had been a major bull's-eye for the nationwide civil rights movement for several years, but the battles seemed to come and go in spurts. Whether it was school integration, buses or public parks, Birmingham constantly seemed to be on the wrong side of the issue, but inevitably either cooler heads or federal law would prevail and things would move along to the next struggle.

At the same time this was going on, the Birmingham Chamber of Commerce decided to fight back with its own public relations campaign, heralded by the slogan "It's Nice to Have You in Birmingham." Irony of ironies, one of the individuals charged with promoting this new program was Commissioner of Public Safety Eugene "Bull" Connor. His official statement on the front page of the *Birmingham News* read, "May your visit in our city be a pleasant one. If you should have any problems, please contact one of our officers for help or advice. You will find them courteous and anxious to help you."

By April 2, 1963, Connor was probably feeling a bit less charitable. The citizens had earlier voted to change Birmingham's long-standing commission form of government to a more reasonable mayor and council form. Connor ran against former lieutenant governor Albert Boutwell for mayor and lost handily. The new city government was set to take over on April 15. However, as someone once said, you cannot accept something until the giver lets go of it, and on that date, the existing city commission refused to give up its position. The city government was in turmoil, with no one who could truly be said to be in charge.

Whether by accident or design, this was exactly when civil rights leader Martin Luther King and his minions came to town to take on the issue of desegregating Birmingham's restaurants, lunch counters and department stores (among other things). On April 3 and 4, demonstrators staged a sit-in at the Britt's—until recently, Newberry's—lunch counter and were summarily arrested. Fearing similar repercussions, Loveman's chose to close its lunch counter, as did Pizitz, Kress and Woolworth's. The rest of that spring and early summer was taken up by one demonstration after another, with Connor giving his police force in particular, and Birmingham in general, a black eye with the tactics he used to squelch such uprisings. In an argument that would be repeated under varying circumstances over the next fifty years, Connor continued to state that he was simply enforcing the law—which indeed he was—and that if it were not for "outside agitators," Birmingham could handle its own problems peacefully.

A boycott of the downtown stores by African Americans finally had the desired result. By May 10, the stores had unanimously agreed to desegregate the lunch counters, restrooms, fitting rooms and drinking fountains. There would also be more African American employees in visible positions; as we saw a little earlier, Loveman's had never been ashamed of honoring its African American workers, but there were still calls for more of them to be placed as sales clerks and so on.

As with most such struggles for change, which never seem to be easy, the individuals who got the most media attention were the ones who made the most noise. That applied equally to both sides of the issue, each of which had "representatives" who did not speak for the views of their respective compatriots. In the case of the civil rights demonstrators, some of them did not necessarily subscribe to King's policy of nonviolence, and in at least one incident, the entire Loveman's building was consumed in a riot. Such activities were not condoned, but that did not prevent them from occurring.

On the other side, the battles in Birmingham brought out the worst in those who proudly considered themselves white supremacists. One of these, most important for our Loveman's discussion, was a certain Edward R. Fields, who formed what he called the National States' Rights Party and, for several weeks during the hottest part of the 1963 summer, mimeographed crudely typed broadsheets he termed the *Birmingham Daily Bulletin*. These

As one of the most important downtown businesses, Loveman's became a particular target for the growing civil rights movement in the early 1960s. In the background, notice the unintentionally ironic chamber of commerce banner proclaiming "It's Nice to Have You in Birmingham." *Rebecca Dobrinski collection.*

would be passed out on sidewalks in front of the downtown businesses to anyone who could be persuaded to take one, and from them we can glean just what sort of fight Loveman's and its brethren were facing. (It is significant that Loveman's chose to preserve copies of these hate-filled rantings in its archives, obviously realizing they might be valuable historical records in the future.) Be forewarned that some of Fields's remarks are difficult to stomach today, but they are necessary to expose just what was going on along those downtown streets.

Although there had no doubt been earlier issues, the first one in Loveman's collection was dated Thursday, July 25. After praising Cecil McGlohon, manager of the Alabama Theatre, for having three African Americans arrested who were trying to buy tickets and enter the venue, Fields warned, "The managers of Loveman's, Britt's, Pizitz, Woolworth's and Kresses [*sic*] have been telling people all week that they cannot arrest Negro sit-ins and also that Boutwell took all Segregation laws off the books. The truth is that they can still arrest anyone who trespasses where they are not wanted or refuse to leave after warning." Under another headline of "Loveman's Victory," Fields wrote:

Last Tuesday we published the news that Loveman's had either fired or removed the White cashier in the lunch room. Negro waitresses were collecting the money. Yesterday the White girl was quickly given her job back and her station placed back where it was before. Patriots who phoned into Loveman's protesting her removal were told that the White girl was on vacation, others were told she was sick and was not laid off. We wish they would agree on one story and stick to it.

A few days later, Fields decided to print a letter addressed to Loveman's president Paul Dowd from a disgruntled customer. As Fields claimed, "Our people cannot trade with those who are helping Martin Luther King destroy our way of life." The letter read:

This I find about the hardest thing I ever had to do. I have hoped against hope, ever since this horrible mess started, that your store would cater to the class of business you have maintained through the years.

It is very hard for people who have maintained, and depended on, their charge accounts since the early 1930s to make the move that is necessary at this point, that of closing out their accounts. I am also closing my account at Pizitz, which has also been of long standing.

Should the time come when you find desirable White customers more profitable to your business, and the air can be cleared of the odor that will linger and prevail, perhaps some of your better customers will return.

It is probably important to jump in here and quickly point out that obviously this person was not speaking for the vast majority of Loveman's customers, or else that would have been the end of the store and these would be the closing paragraphs of the book. That being said, it caused Fields and his fellow travelers to go into an apoplectic fit on July 30 when the lunch counters—these seemed to be the cause du jour—were integrated at Loveman's, Pizitz, H.L. Green, S.H. Kress, Britt's and Woolworth's. As Fields raved almost incoherently, "These stores are the first in Alabama to mix! BLACK day in history! This is the day White people were stabbed in the back! God save the good people of Alabama!"

Fields claimed that the *Birmingham News* and *Birmingham Post-Herald* were deliberately suppressing the names of the stores that had desegregated. In a follow-up to his agitated report above, he wrote:

Burn the names of these stores into your mind. Never forget these stores which joined hands with Martin Luther King to destroy our way of life. No decent, self-respecting Whiteman [sic] will have anything to do with these mongrelized stores. They have Negroes in their White ladies' restrooms, dressing rooms, and today they want us to sit down and eat. Please help us by telling your friends who our enemies are. Don't let these two New York–owned newspapers stop us from spreading the names of these stores to all the people of Birmingham.

The last heard of Fields was on July 31, when, in a gesture often overlooked by historians, he and his picketers were arrested by the same Birmingham police officers who had earlier turned their fire hoses on the civil rights demonstrators. As his foe, the *Birmingham News*, described the day's events:

At noon, Dr. Fields jaywalked across 19th Street between Second and Third Avenues North, carrying a huge placard. He began parading outside Britt's. "This store serves Negroes," one side of the sign read. The other side listed names of six stores that integrated their lunch counters Tuesday.

Police Capt. Glenn Evans approached Dr. Fields and asked him if he had a permit to parade. "I thought an ordinance was recently passed permitting six or more persons the right to demonstrate in front of a store," Dr. Fields replied. He pulled a small Confederate flag from his pocket and started waving it as Evans placed him under arrest and put him in a patrol car.

While this was going on, two other persons, one carrying a large placard and the other waving a huge Confederate flag, picketed Woolworth's across the street. The two men were arrested also, but the flag-bearer refused to surrender his flag. Evans and two other officers struggled with the man for several minutes before wresting the flag from him.

Besides helping explain just how the Confederate flag went from being a beloved historical symbol to its present charred reputation, these incidents seemed to close the chapter—and this chapter, too—on Loveman's direct involvement. It is true that the bombing of the Sixteenth Street Baptist Church the following September pretty much shook to their senses anyone who was not already convinced that times had changed, and African Americans would face still more bloody battles in their fight for the right to vote, but as far as Loveman's, Pizitz and the other downtown stores were concerned, it was all a moot point now. They, and practically everyone who did not share Edward Fields's views, were ready to put it all behind them and concentrate on the future instead of dwelling on the past.

Chapter 6

BUSINESS IS BOOMING

C onsidering everything that had taken place during his tenure, perhaps it should not be too surprising that in September 1964, Paul Dowd announced that he was leaving the office of Loveman's president. His replacement would be John F. Breyer, who up until that time had been merchandise manager of City Stores' Maison Blanche operation in New Orleans. Breyer and Loveman's proved to be a terrific fit for each other; so successful were his first few months as president that before a year had passed, Breyer was simultaneously named a vice-president of the whole City Stores company.

It was a golden era for City Stores in general. Between October 1964 and October 1965, the company's profits, for all of its 132 stores representing various chains across the country, were up nearly three times what they had been for the same period the year before, totaling $3,175,000 (a hefty sum in 1960s dollars, to be sure). City Stores was a mighty vessel in American retailing, and John Breyer, as vice-president, would shoulder considerable responsibility in sailing that ship.

His new vice-presidential position would continue to be second place to Breyer's duties in keeping Loveman's in the forefront of the public's consciousness. With the recent unpleasantness behind it, Loveman's embarked on a series of promotions—some to become annual traditions, some to be tried only once—that would prevent things from ever getting dull behind the corner clock.

One such event for several years was the "Best of Europe Import Fair," a sort of World's Fair in miniature, during which time the hottest new styles from the other side of the Atlantic would be on display. And speaking of displays,

Loveman's employees were always putting on mini-shows to entertain the customers or each other. Here, in May 1964, a group of ersatz Beatles get their yeah, yeah, yeah on while Del Chambordon accompanies them. *John Lehman collection.*

the annual salute to Europe inspired what were probably the most elaborate non-Christmas decorations ever to appear on the exterior of the Loveman's building. Surviving photos show the changing displays of more than one year, including one set of enormous globe-shaped clocks that lined both sides of the building, each set to show the current time in a different European city.

To examine Loveman's newspaper ads of the period, it seemed there was always some sort of special event in the offing, no matter how much it might stretch credibility. But whatever other events crowded the calendar, Christmas continued to be the biggest of all big deals each year. By 1965, Loveman's—the other downtown stores too, to be honest—had turned the entire season into even more than it had been. Kicked off by the lighting of the giant living Christmas tree in Woodrow Wilson Park on the day after Thanksgiving, Loveman's joined in the celebration (or should that be "sellabration"?) of the most joyous time of the year. One of the newspaper ads for that year spelled out just what could be found in the store:

• *See our Animated Windows, where the little creatures of the forest prepare for Christmas (19th Street windows).*

Above: For several years, an annual highlight was the Best of Europe Import Fair. In preparation, Dixie Neon is here installing giant clocks giving the hour in various time zones throughout the world. *Dixie Neon collection.*

Left: In the late 1950s and early 1960s, Loveman's annual holiday slogan was "The Christmas Tree Store," and this catalogue cover took that description literally. *Author's collection.*

• *Bring your little angels in to see Santa—he has a gift for each child.
Third Floor.*
• *The children's very own "Secret Shop" is on the Third Floor—where
they can plan their own gift surprises. All gifts are at piggy bank prices. No
adults allowed!*
• *See the "Yuletide Elf" animated show on our Third Floor, where the
"Little Snow People" make preparation for Christmas.*

The first and last of those items proved that the venerable competition
between Loveman's and Pizitz was alive and well, as Pizitz had unveiled
its new walk-through Christmas display called the Enchanted Forest the
previous season. By gum and by Kringle, if Pizitz's customers could immerse
themselves in a world of snowy trees and animated animals, Loveman's
could respond by having similar scenes in both the windows *and* on the third
floor. Take *that*, you pointy-eared Pizitz pixies, you.

John Breyer certainly had plenty of reason to be jolly that Christmas
season. On December 1, 1965, while publicly presenting the third-quarter
financial statement for City Stores, Breyer used the opportunity to announce
an unprecedented three-year, $7 million expansion program for Loveman's
that was going to make the chain even bigger than anyone had dreamed.
He revealed that the company was negotiating a lease for a location on the
western side of Birmingham and that plans were underway for a similar
encroachment into the city's eastern edges. Both stores, west and east, were
expected to be two-story buildings and open in 1967 and 1968, respectively.
In addition, construction had been rather quietly underway on a new
Loveman's in Huntsville, with a planned March 1966 grand opening.

Asked about Loveman's plans to send out tendrils into other Alabama
cities, Breyer remained a bit coy. "We feel Loveman's is a fine store in a
very good community and that it should grow with the city," he told the
press. "When we are adequately serving the Birmingham area, we'll go
beyond Birmingham in Alabama again." Breyer's words were echoed a few
days later when City Stores president Isadore Newman II paid one of his
frequent visits to the company's Alabama outlet. "We are enthusiastic about
the atmosphere and business climate and about the people here," he told the
same reporters Breyer had faced earlier the same week. He and Breyer also
hinted that Loveman's was going to take steps toward improving the ever-
growing parking problem downtown.

Actually, Loveman's had already been doing something about getting
cars out of the parallel parking lanes. The northeast corner of Second

The view from Loveman's mezzanine was always spectacular, no matter what time of year it was. *Author's collection.*

Avenue North and Eighteenth Street, in the olden days, had been the site of Birmingham's post office. It had moved to Fifth Avenue North by the onset of the Depression, and the old structure had been demolished and removed during projected plans to build a huge new Burger-Phillips store on the spot. Economics squashed that dream, and the corner became a parking lot.

At some undetermined point in history, but probably during the 1950s, the ground-level lot had been replaced by a two-story parking structure shared jointly by Loveman's and the Alabama Theatre. It did not provide hundreds and hundreds of parking spaces, but it was certainly an improvement over driving around the block for a half hour, hoping to find someone backing out of a space along the sidewalk. Loveman's offered an hour of free parking with each purchase of three dollars or more at the store, giving yet another incentive. The area underneath the parking deck became the home to some of downtown's most fondly remembered businesses, including Dixie Cream Donuts, a Krystal hamburger stand (on the corner), a toy and novelty store, Joe Rumore's Record Rack and several others. At the time Loveman's future plans were announced in 1965, the parking structure was largely ignored, but we will soon be seeing how it was going to figure prominently into the upcoming scheme of things.

Another event that would not intersect with Loveman's saga for many more years occurred during the summer of 1965, when suddenly Britt's was bounced out and Newberry's reclaimed its original building as if it had never left. Just like why Britt's had replaced Newberry's in the first place, no particular reason was given for this new turn of events, but soon Britt's was

This two-story parking deck had long been shared by Loveman's and the Alabama Theatre; its ground level housed many fondly remembered downtown businesses, including Krystal, Dixie Cream Donuts and Rumore's Record Rack. *Dixie Neon collection.*

just a vague memory for those who happened to notice it during its three years next door to Loveman's. Yes, I know you are burning with curiosity about why I keep bringing up the goings-on in that building, but you'll just have to trust me that it will pay off eventually. Just hang on and keep reading!

Now, back to the story at hand. On March 3, 1966, the new Loveman's in Huntsville opened right on schedule. It is somewhat odd that the publicity for that grand opening—at least in Birmingham—made it very clear that it was the last Loveman's planned for outside its home city. It was also significant that the Huntsville store was the first Loveman's to be connected with a mall rather than a downtown area or an open-air shopping center. In fact, so novel was the concept of a mall in north Alabama that the new development in Huntsville was known simply as "The Mall." (Even when Birmingham's first example of mall mania, Eastwood Mall, had opened in 1960, newspaper reporters felt obliged to write articles explaining just what a "mall" was.)

This was also the first Loveman's to incorporate the ten-year-old logo into its exterior signage, including the graceful script L. Inside, however, it would be the same classy Loveman's customers had come to expect, although scaled down to fit inside a typical mall store. The news articles gave the details:

> *Most of the store will be devoted to women's fashion. A big Junior Colony Shop that will appeal to teenagers, and the Camellia Room where imported dresses and designer models will be sold, are two unique sections.*

Loveman's third branch store opened in 1966 in Huntsville's new shopping center known simply as The Mall. *Dixie Neon collection.*

The Camellia Room is carpeted, has elegant crystal fixtures, mirrored columns, luxurious fitting rooms. A VIP shop for men has brick floors, paneled walls and antique tables to display the men's styles.

There are departments with fine linen, draperies, crystal, china, furniture, toys, housewares, shoes, cosmetics and accessories. A maternity shop, infants' department and sub-teen department are also in the store.

The grand opening ceremony certainly got the new store off to a good start. It was reported that thousands of Huntsville denizens showed up for the 10:00 a.m. ribbon cutting by Mayor Glenn Hearn, and their ranks swelled later in the day when employees of NASA and Redstone Arsenal ended their normal workdays. "Although special access roads had been cut to allow traffic to enter Loveman's parking lot easily," the account read, "it required seven policemen to direct the traffic jam of customers who came to attend the ceremonies and shop." Such a statement might make one wonder how the whole mall—The Mall, remember—was going to handle the influx of cars, but Loveman's was the first store to open in the new complex. The other fifty-nine stores of The Mall would not open until March 24.

The paint had barely had time to dry in Huntsville before big news was again being made in Birmingham. This time, in July 1966, Loveman's announced that it would be a major anchor of a new mall development to be known as Piccadilly Square, at the corner of U.S. Highway 11 and Weibel Drive in the area where Fairfield and Midfield came together. Piccadilly Square was to cover some nine vast acres, and Loveman's end of the complex would consist of a two-story building with 102,000 square feet of retail space. An opening during 1968 was announced—but as we shall see at the beginning of the next chapter, delays very nearly pushed that into the next decade.

Meanwhile, was the old original downtown Loveman's feeling a bit of sibling rivalry due to the arrival of all these new kids on the block? Perhaps, but there was still plenty going on to show that the company was not going to neglect its flagship store. In February 1967, Loveman's welcomed Maureen O'Sullivan—the movies' Jane to Johnny Weissmuller's Tarzan three decades earlier—as commentator for one of its frequent fashion shows. In her honor, Loveman's display artist (and protégée of Joe Apolinsky) Marian "Teeny" Brannon created a special table decoration depicting a miniature Tarzan set.

This was just a prelude to the big eightieth anniversary blowout, which had gradually been moved back on the calendar from the traditional May 1 date to coincide with the arrival of AEA Week. The theme for the 1967 celebration was "Happiness Is Youth Week," trading on the slogan made famous by the *Peanuts* comic strip. Each day of AEA Week brought new guests to Loveman's various departments. Singers Freddie Cannon and the Gants performed in the record shop; Frank Shicca presented "the new, young look in footwear" in the shoe department; University of Alabama football players Ray Perkins, Cecil Dowdy and Ken Stabler signed autographs in the Store for Men; *Seventeen* fashion model Terry Reno appeared in fashion shows on the second floor; Yardley's of London sent fashion counselor Beverly Hudgins to conduct daily classes in "the London Look"; trainer Johnny Wells and his pride and joy, Herman the Wonder Dog, put on their act on the third floor; Buster Brown shoes

There was entertainment for everyone during Youth Week (aka AEA Week) in 1967, ranging from rock bands to fashion shows to Cousin Cliff to Herman the Wonder Dog. *Author's collection.*

85

sponsored old-time silent movies in the Children's Shop on the third floor; and long-ago Loveman's employee "Cousin Cliff" Holman, by then the biggest kids' TV personality in town, returned for one of his many such visits to emcee the Buster Brown Fashion Show.

Another annual springtime event was the Camellia Awards Fashion Show. From the late 1950s throughout the 1970s, Loveman's was a major participant in this fundraiser of the Linly Heflin Unit. Just what did that entail? Well, the Linly Heflin Unit is still an active part of Birmingham's education scene, but perhaps the thank-you note in its 1967 program will explain it all:

> *Through the courtesy of Loveman's the proceeds of this Annual Fashion Show are given to the Linly Heflin Scholarship Fund. The Linly Heflin Unit has established a charitable educational tax-exempt fund to give scholarships to worthy, ambitious Alabama girls to further their education in Alabama colleges.*
>
> *The Linly Heflin Unit has given scholarships to over 775 Alabama girls, the total fund being well over $176,000. During 1965–66, scholarships were given for the following schools: Alabama College, Auburn University, Birmingham-Southern College, Samford University, Jacksonville State University and the University of Alabama. The Linly Heflin Unit appreciates your support.*

More big news was forthcoming in October 1967. Following through on the hints given the previous year, Loveman's announced that the old two-story parking deck at the corner of Second and Nineteenth would soon make way for a huge multilevel parking deck capable of housing four hundred automobiles at once. The new deck would not only occupy the space of the old one but would also mean the demolition of the five-story Bell Building that fronted on Second Avenue. Yes, that was the same building where Birmingham's telephone exchange had been rendered useless by Loveman's 1934 fire. The phone company had long since moved to other quarters, and the Bell Building was occupied by Carleton Furs, whose huge painted advertising sign loomed over the two-story parking deck.

Real estate agent William P. Engel added that Loveman's long-term lease on the property would commence in April 1970, although construction could begin sooner if possession of the property could be obtained from the various lessees currently occupying the street level. John Breyer pointed out that it would be the largest multilevel self-parking facility in Jefferson

This newspaper graphic illustrated how Loveman's proposed new four-story parking deck would dwarf the old two-level deck; as finally built, it also meant the demolition of the Bell Building, which by this time was home to Carleton Furs. *Marion Breyer collection.*

County and used that point to justify the company's official position: "We feel suburban shopping center developments are good and important to a metropolitan area," he said, "but every city must have a strong downtown area, and Loveman's is striving to make downtown Birmingham of greater service to the entire community with these newly planned developments."

Speaking of the suburbs, there was news concerning that angle too. Construction was to begin shortly on that new mall development out on the Fairfield/Midfield border, the one to be called Piccadilly Square. Well, by October 1967 the name had been changed to Western Hills Mall, and the construction phase was to be completed within eighteen months. Indeed, the groundbreaking was held on November 8, with a projected opening date of February 1969.

That timetable would prove to be susceptible to change. In fact, just days short of a year later—on October 15, 1968—groundbreaking ceremonies were held for *another* mall on that end of town, and it would contain a Loveman's store that had not even been on the radar when all the ambitious future plans were drawn up. West Lake Mall, as it would be known, was to be a 350,000-square-foot shopping destination a mile and a half southwest

Construction on Western Hills Mall and its anchor store, Loveman's, got underway in late 1968. Visiting the site, perhaps for the groundbreaking, are (left to right) Jerry Sklar, John Breyer and Bill Spoor. *Marion Breyer collection.*

of downtown Bessemer, fronting U.S. Highway 11. Loveman's would be one of the three anchor stores, in good company with Sears and W.T. Grant.

The major effect the West Lake Mall development would have on Loveman's history was the announced plan to close the downtown Bessemer store—which, you will recall, had been the first Loveman's branch to open— at the same time the new location opened. Breyer was quoted by the press as saying he was particularly pleased that "the staff nucleus for the new store will come from the skilled and experienced personnel at the present Loveman's in downtown Bessemer."

Like the recent Huntsville store, the West Lake Mall Loveman's would be putting more emphasis on women's fashion than any other department; in fact, the women's area was to take up half of the entire space. The other half would be divided between men's and boys' fashions, gifts, stationery, china, glass, silverware and so on. "Two brilliantly lighted signs will blaze the Loveman's name impressively," the reporter noted. "There will be two entrances to the store, a major entrance from the mall itself and a second from the parking lot."

While heavy equipment moved the dirt around at both the West Lake Mall and Western Hills Mall sites, things continued to move downtown as well. The 1968 Christmas season arrived on schedule, and hark! It heralded a new tradition that would last the rest of Loveman's lifespan.

Over at Pizitz, the Enchanted Forest had continued to grow in size and scope each year, augmenting its original animated animals with tableaux depicting Santa's elves at work making toys, grooming the reindeer and getting the fat guy ready for his big night. Loveman's apparently decided to fight Pizitz's mechanical Santas with the real live article, and beginning on December 2, youngsters from ages four to eight could troop to the downtown store's balcony restaurant for "Breakfast with Santa." Nothing could say it better than the newspaper ad that announced this new concept in fine dining:

> *What a treat! Imagine having breakfast with Santa! Well, that's what's going to happen December 2 through December 21. Children from 4 to 8 are invited to a special Christmas party. Santa will be there, with Birmingham's own Cousin Cliff; music, hot chocolate, Sugar Frosted Flakes and vanilla ice cream, Christmas cookies and more—and not a single mommie or daddy is allowed. The breakfasts begin at 9:15, Monday through Saturday. Parents are welcome to shop in the store during the breakfast—it will last 45 minutes—and pick up their children afterward.*

Before we continue, take just a moment to get the mental image of Santa and Cousin Cliff handing kids back over to their parents after forty-five minutes of plying them with hot chocolate, Sugar Frosted Flakes, ice cream and Christmas cookies. Many moms and pops were probably not saying "ho ho ho" at that point, although some other expressions might have come to their minds. The point was, Loveman's had come up with a winner, but one important element was left out of the description above.

Besides Santa and good ol' Cuz, a third member of this holiday hoedown came straight from the bookkeeping department. Yes, Del Chambordon was still hamming it up for any special event the store presented, but when she first became "Twinkles," Santa's number one elf, it was obvious this was the role she was born to play. Due to her mature features but diminutive stature, kids assumed she really was an elf. It takes more than looks to charm an audience, though, so Twinkles had another trick up her sleeve. Before the breakfast began, she would get things off to a rousing start by descending the stairs that led from the mezzanine to the ground floor, hefting her accordion

Beginning in 1968, Loveman's "Breakfast with Santa" programs featured the inimitable cast of Dave Campbell (alias St. Nick), Cousin Cliff Holman and Del "Twinkles" Chambordon. *Del Chambordon collection.*

and belting out a loud rendition of "Santa Claus Is Comin' to Town." It never failed to get the crowd in the proper mood.

And what about the main man, the jolly old elf, St. Nick in the flesh? Unknown to most of the audience, under the red suit and white beard was a Birmingham broadcasting personality who was as famous in his own right as Cousin Cliff was to the youngsters. Dave Campbell was a longtime WAPI radio host, often credited with pioneering today's omnipresent call-in talk radio format with his nighttime program *The People Speak.* He seemed to have a particular knack for portraying Santa Claus, as he also did so each afternoon on WAPI-TV, reading letters from viewers and reminding them to always leave some raisins for Rudolph along with the milk and cookies. At Loveman's, Campbell restricted his Clausing to the breakfast program and was definitely not the same Santa who sat in the toy department the rest of the day, hoisting kid after kid onto his knee. The team of Campbell, Cousin Cliff and Twinkles was an unbeatable combination, and though Cliff abruptly took his show off WAPI-TV in September 1969 to help start a new TV station in Anniston, even that could not stop him from returning annually to participate in this most enjoyable annual ritual.

Some of those kids were probably just coming down off their sugar high in April 1969 when John Breyer held another press conference to bring everyone up to date on Loveman's various projects in the works. He spent quite a bit of time explaining the ongoing remodeling of the downtown store and how that continued to demonstrate the company's faith in that retail district. The forthcoming parking deck—still more than a year and a half away—was further proof, if anyone was asking.

Then the discussion turned to the two mall stores, Western Hills and West Lake, that were under construction simultaneously. Even in hindsight, it seems strange that a single department store would plan two branches so relatively close together, and apparently that thought was on the reporters' minds in 1969 too. "We need them," he explained in simple enough terms. "The store in the mall at Bessemer will replace our store in downtown Bessemer, which just isn't adequate for our needs. We want each one of our branches to offer the full scope of Loveman's services tailored to each area in which they operate."

That said, he elaborated that the two new branches would not be so much alike as to render each other redundant. The West Lake Mall store would encompass 36,000 square feet and be more of a specialty store, whereas the one at Western Hills would take in 115,000 square feet and be more of the full-line type store for which Loveman's was known. The article ended with a tantalizing glimpse into Loveman's future:

> Loveman's plans do not stop with the construction of these new facilities. Their plans do not even end with spending four million dollars. Breyer smiled as he said it:
>
> "When you start growing or expanding, you've got to keep growing and expanding."
>
> He repeated plans for an eastern store and another possible site and added, "We can't say much about these, for the transactions aren't complete yet. But they're in the works."

The first of all these new plans came to pass on October 29. The West Lake Mall store, which had been started later than the one at Western Hills, opened first. Also as Breyer had promised, Saturday, October 25, had been the final day of operation for the downtown Bessemer Loveman's. Gordon Hunt, who had been acting as manager of that older store for two years, took on the same responsibilities for the new West Lake enterprise, which was stated as having three times as much space. On the same day as the mall opening, Breyer announced the advancement of general accountant and assistant controller Jerry Sklar, a ten-year veteran of Loveman's, to the position of manager of Alabama store operations. Sklar would be playing an increasingly important role during the following ten years. In October 1969, though, no one could have predicted that the coming decade would be Loveman's last.

Chapter 7

THE LOVEMAN'S
DEATH MARCH

When Loveman's opened for its first day of business after the 1970 New Year celebration, most likely none of the employees or executives, or for sure the customers, realized that they were embarking on a ten-year journey that was not going to end well for the venerable old Birmingham institution. At that point, the skies were clear and there was no reason to believe the 1970s would be any different from the other new decades Loveman's had faced.

In fact, there was almost unprecedented ballyhoo surrounding the opening of the newest Loveman's, the Western Hills Mall store, on March 11, 1970. Actually, Loveman's was fashionably late to that particular party; the rest of the mall, anchored at the other end by JCPenney, had opened in January, but Loveman's took a bit longer to be ready. Dixie Neon was once again responsible for the signage and this time almost got the proportions of the giant script L correct. It was especially attractive on the version that loomed over the entrance from the interior of the mall, with the script L outlined in a gentle emerald-green glow and the rest of the Loveman's name in white backlit lettering.

Although the fortunes of Western Hills Mall have been in somewhat of a decline in recent years, let no one doubt that when it opened in 1970, it was truly a magnificent shopping experience—a western mirror to Eastwood Mall on the other side of town. The day before the grand opening, John Breyer took reporters on a guided tour of the new facility, which would be the largest of any of the Loveman's branches.

"Outside these doorways are more than 250,000 shoppers," he pointed out, "in West Birmingham, Fairfield, Midfield, Bessemer, et cetera—the whole

This double-page spread in the *Birmingham News* announced the advent of Loveman's newest branch, the Western Hills Mall store, in March 1970. *Author's collection.*

Western Hills Mall's fortunes have been in somewhat of a decline in recent years, but when it opened in 1970, it was truly a showcase. *Author's collection.*

western area of Jefferson County. These are the customers we're looking for with this new facility." He also commented on the extravagant use of different colors throughout the store. "What we're doing here," he explained, "is trying to create different little areas of excitement within the store—with the gay colors, the new and novel merchandise—all those things are aimed at making a shopping tour of the new Loveman's a rewarding experience."

Yet the downtown store was still the company's pride and joy, and just over a month after Western Hills came a-ridin' into Birmingham's western hills, construction began on the long-promised parking deck adjacent to the old original. On April 20, demolition began on the Bell Building and the parking deck in which Loveman's and the Alabama Theatre shared joint custody. That also meant the end of the line for the thirteen small shops that crowded underneath the old deck, although it was promised this would be compensated by having retail space on the ground floor of the new deck too. It was going to be quite some time before either drivers or shoppers would be able to utilize that new space, though.

Again proving its team player status among the downtown retailers, Loveman's signed on as one of the backers of the ambitious "Birmingham Green" project slated to get underway in the spring of 1971. In case you were not paying attention back then, the idea was to clear Twentieth Street, downtown's major thoroughfare, of perceived urban blight and turn it into a more pedestrian-friendly venue landscaped with trees and bushes. With the not surprising encouragement of several women's garden clubs, the presidents of Loveman's, Pizitz, Parisian, Bromberg's and Blach's all pledged their support. While Birmingham Green, as it was

OUR COMPLETE STOCK OF MISSES AND JR. SWIMSUITS

1/3 OFF

Junior swimsuits include cotton bikini, cage and pinafore styles in assorted prints and solids. Sizes 5 to 13. Were 14.00 to 26.00 . . . . 8.99 to 16.99
Misses swimwear includes one and two-piece styles, skimmers and overblouse styles in assorted colors. Sizes 8 to 18 . . . . ⅓ off
Misses and Junior Sportswear, second floor—Downtown, Bessemer, Western Hills

Famous make swimsuits in prints and solids **50% off**
Save on one and two-piece swimsuits from one of our most famous makers. Sizes 8 to 20. Now 8.49 to 9.99 were 17.00 to 20.00
Misses Bowl Sportswear, street floor—Downtown, Bessemer.
Western Hills, Montgomery, Huntsville

LOVEMAN'S

Shop Downtown Monday 10:00 AM until 9:30 PM—Bessemer and Western Hills 10:00 AM until 9:00 PM

In the summer of 1970, Loveman's business was growing while swimsuits were getting smaller—not that there was anything wrong with either of those things. *Author's collection.*

94

finally completed, fulfilled all of its stated goals, privately many retailers accused it of hastening the coming decline in downtown business. Not that it was unattractive, but it effectively eliminated parking along the street and forbade the kind of signage that had formerly made stores and restaurants so easy to locate. Since Loveman's sat a block away from the new development, it probably was not affected as directly as some others, but slowly and surely the suburban malls and shopping centers were sapping the energy that had once powered the downtown retail machine.

At about the same time the first shovels of dirt were being turned over on Twentieth Street, John Breyer announced that director of operations Jerry Sklar was being moved up the corporate ladder to vice-president of Loveman's. His importance to the company would continue to build over the next few years, but the news of his new appointment prompted at least one touching letter from an erstwhile competitor:

> *I was delighted to read of your appointment as Vice President-Administration for Loveman's. I know it is a promotion of which you can be justifiably proud.*
>
> *Despite some of our frequent kidding, I did want you to know that I am well aware of the fine job you have done for Loveman's. Again, my sincere congratulations.*
> *Sincerely,*
> *Michael Pizitz*

Perhaps it was also a sign of the times a-changing (again?) that the store newsletter, the *Loveman's Ledger*, during 1971 began carrying more and more short features dealing with employees receiving rewards—a generous five dollars each—for helping apprehend shoplifters and other miscreants. Unfortunately, this trend in crime would prove to be a permanent houseguest, but other "modern" developments were certainly more temporary. A July 1971 issue contained the following paragraph about a downtown store feature that must have come and gone rather quickly: "The Computer Handwriting Analysis machine has created a lot of excitement around here. It's a very new thing and our Stationery Department was the first to display such a machine. With a constant 'peep, peep, peep' it sounds like wild birds heading south for the winter."

On November 15, about the time the real birds were heading south, the much-anticipated four-hundred-car parking deck opened after months of work and even more years of waiting. John Breyer and City Councilmen Don Hawkins and Russell Yarbrough handled the cutting of the ceremonial

Just in time for the 1971 Christmas shopping season, John Breyer cut the ribbon opening the new Loveman's parking deck. Hopefully, people were concentrating on navigating the ramp too much to notice the horribly deformed rendition of Loveman's trademark script L. *Marion Breyer collection.*

ribbon, which once again dipped into *Peanuts* slogan territory with the motto "Happiness is a place to park." (That's a topic Charlie Brown and Snoopy likely never thought about.) Over the Second Avenue ramp entrance to the deck was a sign bearing possibly the most deformed rendition of the script L ever seen on an official Loveman's property.

Along the way, Loveman's never made it a point to directly address the fact that Pizitz had opened its own parking deck back in 1965, but there did seem to be some efforts to prove that newer was better. At Pizitz, no matter on which level someone parked, they had to take the elevator to enter Pizitz's third floor via the famed "skywalk," passing a fragrant outpost of one of the Pizitz Bake Shops en route. The Loveman's deck strove to make things more convenient, explained the article the day before the opening: "Each level will have an elevator lobby, providing easy access to each floor of Loveman's Store for the Home, itself a four-story structure. Two high speed, sound monitored elevators will serve the new parking facility."

After Breyer announced that part of the new retail space on the deck's ground level had been leased to women's clothier Lane Bryant, the deck was officially opened by having two chauffeur-driven Cadillacs, courtesy of Drennen Motor Company, haul guests up the entrance ramp. It was the culmination of Loveman's contemporary expansion plan.

Those Christmas shoppers who came to take advantage of the parking deck that season could enjoy the newest approach to Loveman's famed animated

96

windows—one of the last of that type that would be seen downtown. With the recent opening of Walt Disney World in Orlando, Florida, on many people's minds, the Loveman's windows brought to life many of the beloved Disney characters. Twenty years later, occasional deteriorating figures from that grand promotion were still turning up occasionally for sale by local antique dealers. The Western Hills Mall store did not go in for animated windows but instead had an enormous cut-out Santa Claus that stretched the width of the exterior façade, looking as if St. Nick were embracing Loveman's in the biggest, warmest hug in history.

With the recent opening of Walt Disney World in Florida, the Fantasyland crew turned out en masse for Loveman's 1971 Christmas season. Disney merchandise flooded the toy department, while animated Disney characters cavorted in the display windows. *Author's collection.*

With all the planned projects now successfully completed, John Breyer announced that he would retire from Loveman's as of May 1, 1972. His replacement as president was Clifford Hoehne, most recently the president of fellow City Stores outlet Lowenstein's in Memphis. Naturally, there was a lot of media attention devoted to how this new arrival was going to fit in with Birmingham and one of its oldest companies:

Citing what he calls the "fantastic" growth of such things as the medical center, civic center and the city's expressways, Hoehne says he is impressed with the Birmingham market and believes that "We are on the verge of a great upsurge in the whole Birmingham area.

"Merchandising is changing because of the demands of a new life style," he says. He cites pants for women and "the whole revolution" in men's apparel and adds, "I think the people are saying 'We're trying to get

more out of life,' and this is reflected in how they dress. The successful department store of the future will reflect the needs of this type of customer."

One project Breyer had left on the drawing board for his successor was that long-hinted-at plan for a Loveman's on the eastern side of Birmingham. With Pizitz comfortably ensconced at Eastwood Mall, there was certainly no chance of Loveman's getting a toehold there. But the articles in May 1972 revealed that a new mall was under development catty-cornered across U.S. Highway 78 from Eastwood. The as-yet-unnamed development would have Loveman's as one of its major tenants, and Hoehne promised, "It won't be the last expansion for Loveman's in a growing Birmingham."

Somewhat surprisingly, little information has survived concerning any goings-on between that point and the opening of the new mall, finally named Century Plaza, on August 4, 1975. But what an impression Loveman's made with its sixth—and, ultimately, final—store. The exterior signage outdid all of its predecessors, with the giant script L this time composed of dozens of "chasing" light bulbs that gave the corporate symbol a shimmering, jewel-like look at night. The newest Loveman's also contained a full-service Gallery Restaurant, complete with cocktail facilities and a liquor license. The restaurant was situated at the eastern end of the entire mall complex, overlooking the traffic on I-20 heading to and from Atlanta.

In fact, Century Plaza was widely believed to be the largest two-story shopping mall between Atlanta and Houston, Texas. The new Loveman's was certainly the largest branch store in the chain, with only the downtown

Loveman's final branch store opened in the new Century Plaza mall during the summer of 1975. *Del Chambordon collection.*

location outclassing it in size. President Hoehne made it sound as if a visit to City Stores' newest pride and joy would be something like dipping into Florida's fabled Fountain of Youth, calling it "a store of exciting shopping adventures. Departments have staged settings with bold splashes of color, dramatic lighting effects and unusual display islands. Loveman's Century Plaza will amuse, excite and delight. Shopping this contemporary store will make you feel younger, just to be inside."

For those who really were young, inside as well as outside, the toy department at the Century Plaza store was singled out for a Merchandising Achievement Award from the toy industry publication *Playthings*. The February 1976 issue described a visit to the Loveman's toy displays, which immediately made it stand out from, say, a Woolworth's or Kmart:

> *As customers enter the department, they are surrounded by clear Lucite cubicles in which toys are displayed. This attractive arrangement can be seen from anywhere on the floor. Loveman's believes in wooing the customers with beautiful things. Accordingly, the cubicles feature dolls from Madame Alexander and stuffed creatures by Steiff and Fable in groupings so charming that they lure shoppers into the section.*

Behind these scenes, Loveman's was beginning to experience an alarmingly frequent turnover of chief executives, especially considering the long tenures of the ones who had served in that office before. Clifford Hoehne was succeeded by Alvin Richer, who resigned in either late 1976 or early 1977 to be replaced by Theodore Bierman of Cincinnati, formerly president of that city's H&S

In contrast to the days when Loveman's exterior glowed with Christmas decorations, by the 1975 holiday season, the ornamentation had been reduced to a few silvery snowflakes. *Rebecca Dobrinski collection.*

Pogue stores. Then, in March 1978, forty-one-year-old Jerry Sklar was booted upstairs from vice-president to president, a move that made him the youngest executive to head Loveman's. It also, as he often points out now, put him in the eventual position of being the captain who was to go down with his ship.

The first dark clouds began to roil over the horizon in July 1979, although most people unaware of the inner workings of a large department store chain might have dismissed them as a mere passing shower. Ominously but honestly, the *Birmingham News* reported:

> *City Stores Inc., parent company of Loveman's stores here, has filed for bankruptcy under a section of the federal Bankruptcy Act that will allow it to continue operating for the time being. Loveman's president Jerry Sklar said today that under the court order, the company will continue to be run by its own corporate management without a receiver or trustee.*
>
> *Sklar said the action is a reorganization and refinancing of the parent company under a New York federal court order. "We are a very viable company and will continue to be," Sklar said, "We plan to continue our normal operations."*

All seemed normal as the 1979 Christmas season made its annual appearance. The employee handbook for that year made no mention of the bankruptcy situation and, in fact, showed that Loveman's was continuing in its usual elegant way. From November 30 through December 18, the "Breakfast with Santa" tradition had its usual run, with Cousin Cliff, Twinkles and Dave "Santa" Campbell putting on their act in the mezzanine restaurant. (By that time, Del Chambordon had moved to the Century Plaza store— much closer to her home on Rugby Avenue—but she eagerly made her way back downtown daily for this enjoyable holiday custom.) In addition, from December 12 to 22, the mezzanine restaurant offered a special dinner menu until 7:30 p.m. for those last-minute shoppers.

Once Loveman's final set of jolly holidays was finished, things rapidly went from merry to not so much. In February 1980, City Stores made the official announcement that it was considering selling the six Loveman's stores to another company if a suitable buyer could be found. City Stores was floundering to keep its head above the bankruptcy waters and, in an effort to downsize and streamline, had already closed the forty-two stores in New York's Franklin Simon chain and the eight-store Richard's chain in the Miami area. All that was left, besides Loveman's, were eight Maison Blanche stores in Louisiana, four Lowenstein's stores in Memphis and forty-five W&J Sloane home furnishings stores.

By late March, it was obvious that Loveman's future was unraveling fast. The Birmingham mayor's office offered to help City Stores find a buyer for Loveman's, particularly the downtown store, but nothing came of that. On March 23, the newspapers announced that Jerry Sklar had been appointed president of the Maison Blanche chain but that he would not leave Birmingham "until my obligations are fulfilled at Loveman's." He maintained that negotiations were ongoing to determine Loveman's fate but that one possibility was that the six locations could be split up and sold to separate buyers, rather than a single company absorbing them all.

Three days later, Sklar was not sounding as optimistic. The general economic recession that had the country in its grip was not the most conducive time to be trying to sell an upscale department store chain, he explained. "The important thing to us is the high interest rates and an uncertain economic situation that make it very difficult to find people who would want to buy the business. Whereas two months ago, it was a different situation. I am positive that the companies we are dealing with are trying to come to grips with the high money cost and uncertainty in the economy, but it has been delayed."

On March 31, the final Loveman's newspaper ads appeared, although there was nothing about them to indicate that significance. They simply ran in their usual size and position, and on April 1, there were no Loveman's ads, period. Instead, the headlines blared that at some point during that month, Loveman's would either be sold or closed; there was no third option. Sklar insisted that no date had been set for any closings and bristled when

After almost a century, this was the final newspaper ad for Loveman's, appearing on March 31, 1980. The next day, headlines would blare that the chain would close within a week, but it actually turned out to be even sooner than that. *Author's collection.*

told Mayor Arrington's office said it had been informed the stores would go out of business the following Saturday. "What is this, is the mayor running Loveman's?" Sklar snapped, the many weeks of stress bubbling to the surface.

As it turned out, with the news leaking whether City Stores wanted it to or not, Sklar and City Stores chairman of the board Jack Farber were obliged to send the following letter to all Loveman's employees on April 2. It needs no further annotation:

> *To all of our Loveman's Associates:*
>
> *We must advise you of our decision to cease operations in the Loveman's stores at the close of business on April 5, 1980. It is not easy or pleasant to discuss plans to terminate Loveman's. However, you are entitled to the reasons for this decision.*
>
> *The Directors and Senior Management of this Company have exhausted all courses of action open to us in an effort to maintain Loveman's operation. No stone was left unturned. However, the strategic plan for the revitalization of City Stores requires that the Company be restructured into a department store division consisting of Maison Blanche of New Orleans and Lowenstein's of Memphis, and a Home Furnishings division consisting of W&J Sloane Fashion Home Furnishings stores. All aspects of the plan, including its effect upon personnel, have been subjected to searching examination by the Planning and Executive Committees. In these deliberations the future of our employees has been of primary concern.*
>
> *We realize how difficult this decision must be for all of you who have labored on behalf of the Company, and we want you to know that your loyalty, dedication and services are deeply appreciated.*
>
> *Your paycheck will be available to you on April 5, 1980. Following closing, some management personnel will be available in the Downtown Birmingham store to answer your questions concerning health insurance coverage, pension rights, references to future employers, as well as other questions that you may have as a result of the decision to terminate operations.*

Indeed, the human drama represented by Loveman's closing was as great a tragedy as the loss of an almost century-old Birmingham institution. It was estimated that the six stores represented nearly seven hundred employees, all of whom would now be out of work. Of the many newspaper articles eulogizing Loveman's, one of the most unusual appeared on April 4. Although the news might well have been eclipsed by the Loveman's unfolding drama, the fact was that on the same day the department stores closed, the legendary A&P grocery store chain was also shutting down all its stores in

Birmingham. This was acutely felt by Tom and Thelma Matchen of East Lake; Tom worked for A&P and Thelma for Loveman's, meaning that both of them were suddenly unemployed as of the same date.

Though Birmingham was going to experience Loveman's absence most often, as the old saying goes, there was much sighing in Huntsville and Montgomery, too. The Montgomery newspaper profiled Mildred Amos, who had the distinction of going to work in the Normandale store on opening day and remaining to become the only original employee still with the store on the last day of business. "I helped open it up, and I'm very sad about Loveman's closing," she said. "Loveman's meant a lot to the neighborhood. I hope some other major department store will come in here."

And so it came to pass. At 6:00 p.m. on April 5, 1980, the cash registers were totaled out for the last time, and Loveman's became part of history. The end had come.

Well…almost.

During the next few weeks, there were spotty newspaper articles concerning what was to be done with the corpse. Most surprising was the April 12 announcement that at least two of the Loveman's stores would not be closed permanently after all but would no longer be operating under that name. Arch rival Pizitz purchased the Century Plaza and Western Hills Mall locations and promised they would reopen the following week. The good news was that Pizitz intended to rehire as many of the employees of those two locations as possible, ensuring that business would continue as usual.

There was also the not-so-little matter of the merchandise that was still housed in the remaining four locations. On April 26,

Between late April and late May 1980, the Loveman's buildings downtown and at West Lake Mall, Huntsville and Montgomery reopened to liquidate the remaining merchandise. This ad is a sad contrast to the ones we have seen throughout this book. *Author's collection.*

And so it all came down to this. At 3:00 p.m. on May 29, 1980, the downtown Loveman's store locked its doors for good. A *Birmingham News* photographer was on hand to capture that bitter moment. *Birmingham Public Library Southern History collection.*

City Stores officials announced that the downtown store and the West Lake Mall, Huntsville and Montgomery branches would reopen for liquidation sales to clear out all the leftover inventory. That was certainly a successful move, as so many people turned out for the final clearance that some had to wait in line for a half hour just to pay for their purchases. That lasted for one frantic month, but at 3:00 p.m. on Thursday, May 29, the doors were again locked, and Loveman's was now really, truly a dead dinosaur.

Well…almost.

Obviously the job of shutting down a company of Loveman's size entailed tying up many loose ends, so a skeleton staff was kept busy during the following weeks just making sure everything was taken care of. Jerry Sklar prepared for his move to New Orleans to take over the presidency of Maison Blanche, but just as he had promised, he would not leave Birmingham until all the work was done.

The fateful day arrived on July 29. On that day, Sklar found on his desk a handwritten letter from his longtime secretary, Mildred Frazier:

> *Jerry: That time has arrived! My last hours at, with, and for Loveman's. It is difficult to realize—but that, too, will come.*
>
> *Your note touched me deeply. Thank you, Jerry, for the expression of your very kind thoughts, and your kindness and generosity through the years. Working with you has meant a great deal to me.*
>
> *You are very fortunate, for you have all the right ingredients for success in any endeavor.*
>
> *Be happy, always.*

And this time, it really was the end.

Chapter 8

BACK FROM THE DEAD, THE SECOND TIME AROUND

W hen the doors were locked after the final clearance sale at Loveman's, it seemed to be anyone's guess as to what should be done with the still-magnificent old building. Plans for its future began swirling about later that same year, but one thing was certain: whatever the building's fate, it obviously was never going to be a department store again. Despite the best efforts of such groups as the Downtown Action Committee, shoppers had been fleeing the city center for the suburban malls and shopping centers for the better part of the previous twenty years. The first of Birmingham's old-line downtown stores to go under was Burger-Phillips, which succumbed in 1975 (although it kept its mall branches open). That was followed by S.H. Kress, across the corner from Loveman's, which gave up in 1978. Pizitz would sell out to Mississippi's McRae's chain at the end of 1986, and the new company elected to close the downtown store in early 1988. Later in 1988, Loveman's other neighbor, Woolworth's, also decided to vacate downtown, so the neighborhood really began to look abandoned by that time. By the early 1990s, the only traditional retailer still doing business downtown was J.J. Newberry, which, as we have seen numerous times, had shared Loveman's fortunes in both good times and bad.

Birmingham News writer Jerry Underwood certainly did his research in the paper's morgue, because in 1990, he came up with the following chronology of the many failed plans to inject life back into Loveman's, somewhat like trying to raise the dead:

> • *In 1980, it was mentioned as a possible site for the Birmingham Public Library. The library board eventually decided to construct a new building across the street from the old library.*

• *There was short-lived talk that same year that it might become the city's new police headquarters building.*

• *A local real estate executive proposed turning the empty building into a trade mart to serve wholesalers. The plan never got off the ground.*

• *There was talk of turning it into an office and retail center, with the Jefferson County School Board occupying the top two floors.*

• *In 1981, developers Nelson Head and Pedro Costa bought the property for $1.3 million and dreamed of turning it into "The Market," a collection of boutiques, food shops, a children's retail area and a conference center. The partnership went bankrupt.*

• *In 1988, a Michigan development company wanted to buy Loveman's and the nearby J.J. Newberry building for luxury condominiums. The plan counted on federal funding the city was unable to obtain.*

Of this boulevard of broken dreams, it was the Costa-Head partnership that almost spelled doom for the very downtown buildings it hoped to revive. Besides Loveman's, the Costa-Head project bought the Alabama Theatre, the S.H. Kress and Burger-Phillips buildings and a few other landmarks in the area. The eventual bankruptcy proceedings meant that all of these historic structures were suddenly in danger of being sold to the highest bidder in order to pay off their mortgages and delinquent taxes, and the Alabama Theatre came uncomfortably close to becoming a parking lot. "For some, the queen looks more attractive dead than alive," the *News* leered at the time, pointing out the priceless antique furnishings and abundance of gold leaf the old movie palace contained. It was only through the dedication of Cecil Whitmire and his Alabama Chapter of the American Theatre Organ Society that the 1927 masterpiece was saved from demolition. Loveman's was a lot less valuable from a collectors' viewpoint, and unfortunately, for most of the 1980s it had no champion of Whitmire's class to come to the rescue.

While downtown was dithering around, out in the southern part of the city there was at least some activity at A.B. Loveman's old mansion on Rhodes Circle. You may recall that A.B. had built his home circa 1900, only getting to enjoy it for sixteen years. A.B.'s widow had resided there until her own death, after which it was occupied by one of the Loveman daughters, Leona Cronheim. At various times since, the structure had been owned by the Salvation Army and served a stint as a girls' lodge, but during the spring of 1984, attorney David Shelby bought the home and turned it into an office complex. (Joseph Loveman's former home next door remained, and still remains, a private residence.)

A.B. Loveman's home on Rhodes Circle, built circa 1900, has today been lovingly restored and serves as the offices for the Shelby-Roden law firm. *Robert Roden collection.*

Shelby's renovation of the edifice certainly reflected a historian's respect for preserving tradition. A newspaper article discussing the project pointed out that the conversion into law offices retained the fireplaces and mantels, the high, beamed ceilings, dark wood wainscoting and the original dining room (turned into a conference room). One of the few outright replacements had to be the substitution of new stained-glass panels in place of some of the original windows that had been stolen during one of the periods the house had sat vacant. "Apparently even the burglars were impressed with the beauty of the house," the paper stated, "since they did the job very carefully, without damaging the house." Today, the former Loveman home continues its second career as the offices of the Shelby-Roden law firm.

If only the 1935 Loveman's store could have attracted such loving attention. The longer it sat abandoned, the worse it looked—and the fact that most of the Loveman signage remained in place, just as it had been on closing day, made the building's deterioration look even sadder. The tall, enclosed bridges that connected the main building to the Store for the Home were encased in a brick structure that continued to bear a fading painted sign advertising the five locations. The dark green metal letters spelling out the store's name still hung on the Third Avenue and Nineteenth Street sides of the building, as rust stains crept across the façade. At some point during

By 1990, the downtown Loveman's was beginning to look more than a little seedy. A well-intentioned project to decorate the glass in the empty display windows with murals did not help wipe away the urban blight. *Author's collection.*

the 1980s, there was a well-meaning but ultimately rather disheartening art project to paint murals on the existing glass of the former display windows, but the final effect was to look more like an abandoned urban neighborhood fraught with graffiti.

One of the few bright spots of that dismal decade was the ultimate rescue and reopening of the Alabama Theatre for special events, initially consisting mostly of organ concerts and the showing of classic movies. These events proved that people were still willing to come downtown after dark—a very visible security presence hired by the theater no doubt helped—and the Alabama made arrangements to use the former Loveman's parking deck, now owned by the city, during such presentations. The irony might have been lost on everyone that the 1900 Loveman home had been reborn, and the 1971 parking deck was being used once again, yet the main store sat unwashed and unloved, the very emblem of urban blight. Would that never change?

On December 16, 1990—a time when, in decades past, Loveman's would have been crowded with Christmas shoppers—the *Birmingham News* broke the story that the city was close to making a deal to buy the building for use as a science museum. The National Bank of Commerce had retained ownership since the Costa-Head debacle and had the building valued at $787,030, with an additional $987,000 value assigned to the 32,900 square feet of land it sat on. Everyone realized, though, that regardless of what had to be paid to acquire the property, the real cash outlay was going to come when it was time to make it livable once again.

The proposed new facility would be the combined homes for the Red Mountain Museum, which specialized in documenting the area's rich mineral and fossil history, and the Discovery Place, a hands-on children's museum. The two disparate enterprises had recently merged, although some elements of each remained in separate locations. The Red Mountain Museum, in particular, overlooked the cut in Red Mountain made by construction of the Elton B. Stephens Expressway (aka Red Mountain Expressway) in the 1960s and 1970s; the museum grounds were decorated with a retired fiberglass brontosaurus that had formerly served as the logo for a Sinclair gas station. Discovery Place was in a residential section of Twenty-second Street South. Combining both under one roof seemed like a good idea—but was Loveman's long-neglected roof too leaky to protect them?

That was one of the first questions the museum staffers needed to answer, so early in the process, a group of them, including exhibits director Lamar Smith and maintenance whiz Bruce Brasseale, made what appeared to be an archaeological expedition into the very bowels of the building. "It was fascinating, but it was very dilapidated," recalls Smith. "It was almost like going back in time; there were a lot of store signs— the pharmacy, shoes, coats—and the signs around the escalators. The mezzanine still had remnants of the beauty shop and elements of the diner. There were tons of keys that no one knew what locks they fitted, and time clocks throughout the place. Some areas looked like they had just been

When the Red Mountain Museum took control of the Loveman's building, one of its first visits revealed five inches of standing water in the former bargain basement. *Bruce Brasseale collection.*

locked up and walked away from, like the print shop on the roof where the artists created all the ads and signs. The most disturbing thing was that the basement had about five inches of water standing in it."

Brasseale concurs with Smith's recollection and has the dimly lit photos to prove it:

> *When we first came in, we walked down the escalator with our flashlights— it was pretty spooky—and we thought the basement floor was waxed, because it was so shiny. But it was five inches of water on 34,000 square feet. It would fill up to the elevators and then level out. It wasn't sludge, either—it was clear, clean underground water. When the power was cut off to the building, of course the pumps stopped working. It took four days to pump it all out.*

Just three days after the initial announcement was made, the Birmingham City Council voted to give Mayor Richard Arrington the power to spend the necessary $1.3 million to buy Loveman's. The newspapers stated this was far below its appraised value but about the same as the National Bank of Commerce had paid when it obtained the building after the Costa-Head mess. No one even wanted to guess at how much it was going to cost to renovate a decaying department store into a spiffy new science museum, but the city did have access to the balance of $5 million that had been raised in a 1984 bond issue specifically for the purpose of building a science museum somewhere—just not necessarily at Loveman's.

Among several hundred other decisions that had to be made was determining just what remnants of the building's past would be preserved. In some cases, it didn't much matter what everyone preferred; there was simply no choice. "There were a lot of store fixtures hung up that just had to be burned off, like the old store sprinkler systems and so on," said Smith. "There was a lot of overhead stuff like that, which just had to be cleaned out and gone." Early on, it was decided to tear out the ceilings and leave the exposed structural elements as part of the teaching atmosphere of a science museum. There was some talk of trying to restore the ornamentation on the massive first-floor columns, but it eventually turned out that would have distracted from the overall new look.

As Smith says:

> *The columns had a very beautiful plaster detailing around them that we talked about replicating, but we were unable to do that. We were able to*

replicate the outside window ornamentation in fiberglass. The escalators were all taken out because they were outdated and there were safety concerns. Since then, though, in 2006 we added one escalator from the second to the third floor, but we had to shut it down because of the nature of children wanting to run up and down.

Removing the escalators was a step that would eventually matter probably only to those who remembered Loveman's in its heyday. Stairs were constructed in the space the escalators formerly occupied, so most people never even noticed they were gone. Since the museum, as finally completed, was going to use only the basement and the first three floors for public areas, the openings for the escalators between the third and fourth floors had to be sealed up. If you ever find yourself on the third floor, take a close look above you, and around the middle of the space you will see the very slight tell-tale signs of a "patch" in the ceiling, a silent monument to the long-gone 1955 escalators.

The Discovery 2000 crew also had their work disrupted because they found they were not alone in the building. No, it was not the ghosts of A.B. Loveman, Moses Joseph and Emil Loeb coming back to haunt them; it was a much more physical presence. "Even during the time we were still draining water out of the building, there were people living in it," Lamar Smith explains. "It was so tough because we would work all day, and then at night they would somehow get in and take the copper wiring off the elevator motors and undo what we had done."

By May 1991, not much progress could be seen outside Loveman's, as most everything was taking place indoors. It was around that time that *Birmingham News* reporter Tom Gordon chose to do a story about people's memories of the long-gone downtown theater and retail district. Naturally, the resulting article focused primarily on Pizitz and Loveman's, and writer Gordon managed to get a representative of each business down to their former turf. Richard Pizitz handled the commentary on the store his grandfather had founded, while Loveman's was eulogized by Del "Twinkles" Chambordon, who got her first glimpse of the building's interior since closing day eleven years before.

Chambordon reacted audibly to the absence of the stairs that once led from the main floor to the mezzanine. Photographer Jerry Ayres captured a melancholy image of Chambordon standing in the once-grand main floor, now little more than a barren concrete slab, and also a much cheerier shot of her in front of the corner clock, which had its hands permanently stopped at 4:50…a.m. or p.m., no one could say.

For a 1994 newspaper feature on downtown's glory days, Del "Twinkles" Chambordon was photographed in the cavernous street floor of Loveman's, which still contained most of the décor that had been there at closing time fourteen years earlier. *Author's collection.*

Many of Loveman's relics, which were scattered throughout the building, the Third Avenue annex and the Second Avenue Store for the Home, were preserved in state-of-the-art archival storage methods, but some things were just too large to be saved. To this day, Bruce Brasseale has pangs of guilt about one of the building's most notable elements that got away. "I admit to being the one who threw away the Loveman's signs that were on the outside," he says. There were actually three sets of the huge green metal letters: one on the Third Avenue side, one on the Nineteenth Street side and one on the Store for the Home. Brasseale says that for a while, the iconic letters were stored in the Discovery 2000 warehouse. "But finally they needed the space, and I was ordered to trash them," he says ruefully. "I thought of taking some of them home with me, but we ended up hauling all of them to the dump."

It did not take long to find out that while the main part of Loveman's, the 1935 section, was the prize, the end had come for the two annexes. It was thought that perhaps the 1917 annex fronting on Third Avenue might be salvageable, since it was the only part of Loveman's that had survived the fire, but the workers soon found that survival did not mean the annex was in the fittest shape of its life. Brasseale explains, "They tested the annex to see if it would hold our weight, but it wouldn't. They put a swimming pool in there and filled it up with water and used that to measure how much the floor moved. They could see the annex was damaged too much to save." It seemed the infamous fire, which was already just a vague memory for Birmingham's older residents, was not yet finished with destroying the building.

Actually, it turned out that the 1917 annex and the Store for the Home were not going to be the only structures in Loveman's neighborhood that would give way to progress. In April 1992, the city made an announcement that will relieve the tension you faithful readers have been enduring for all these pages: you are about to learn why the seemingly unrelated stories of Loveman's and the J.J. Newberry variety store have been intertwining ever since the 1930s. Yes, folks, the Birmingham City Council authorized Mayor Arrington to spend $425,000 to acquire the Newberry's building to help expand the plans for Discovery 2000.

Just how was the spot where Newberry's stood going to be used? No one seemed to know. Arrington had in mind that demolishing the building would make room for an outdoor courtyard. Museum officials had other ideas. The newspaper reported that they "are pushing to use the Newberry's spot as a place to build a $5 million 'Omnimax theater,' an extra-large, dome-shaped movie theater that provides super-realistic visual effects."

There was one minor bit of unfinished business that had to be dealt with before any of these plans could proceed, though—namely, Newberry's was still an operating business and expressed no particular desire to be otherwise. Since the longtime chain did not own the building but leased it (as it had since Clem Melancon had first allowed it to share part of his space), it had no real say-so in what was going to happen. Store manager John Dunn was caught off guard. "I had no earthly idea about this," he told reporters. "The mayor was nice enough to call yesterday to say it would get out in the media today. To tell you the truth, I was totally shocked."

Several city representatives expressed their confidence that Newberry's would remain in business downtown, even though it would have to find a new location. With all the other former stores sitting empty, available space was not going to be an issue. For the time being, Discovery 2000 was having enough to do just trying to figure out what to build and how to pay for it, so Newberry's was not in danger of being closed immediately.

By December 1993, Discovery 2000 had raised $12 million of the estimated $50 million that was going to be needed for the project. Even though the money was not yet there, ambitious plans were still being drawn up. The Omnimax theater was still considered one of the most exciting and ambitious aspects of the new museum complex, more than a year and a half since it had first been mentioned almost as a footnote. A new element introduced into the mix was the idea of an enclosed rainforest environment, with live animals and plants, that would sit inside a sort of greenhouse dome atop Loveman's roof. Just in case any of these drastic changes made veteran city residents nervous, one paragraph of the December 1993 story comfortingly read: "One part of the building will be left unchanged: The outdoor clock at the corner of Third Avenue North and 19th Street, which served as a meeting space for generations of downtown shoppers, still works and will be plugged in soon."

The reprieve Newberry's had enjoyed since the city purchased the building came to an end at 5:30 p.m. on Thursday, January 26, 1995. That signified the final hour of business for the store, and as usual, people were waxing nostalgic about it. The store manager, for his part, demonstrated a remarkable lack of knowledge about his own business by telling the *Birmingham News* that the store was "founded in 1916 by the Newberry family of Birmingham." Thus, he not only got the start of the business confused with the year Louis Saks had built the building to house his dry goods store but also seemed unaware that Newberry's was a national chain, based in the Northeast, that just happened to have outlets in Birmingham. Perhaps he was simply in a state of shock. Unlike the predictions of the optimistic economic developers, Newberry's (by then a branch of McCrory Stores) did not seek a new location downtown.

The city of Birmingham condemned the J.J. Newberry store so it could be demolished to make way for the future McWane Science Center's new IMAX theater. *Author's collection.*

It might have seemed like a further insult that after Newberry's was forced to close, the building stood empty for more than a year before being razed. In March 1996, the walls began to fall; disturbing newspaper photos showed that the store still wore the teal-colored metal sheathing

Meet Me Under the Clock

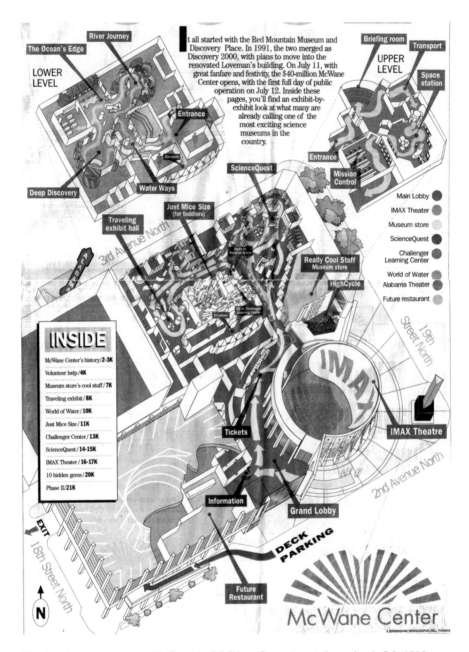

This handy newspaper graphic from the McWane Center's grand opening in July 1998 gave an excellent idea of how the new museum appropriated Loveman's former retail spaces. *Author's collection.*

it had received in its 1961 remodeling and the Newberry's signs were still in place as the heavy equipment chomped away at the structure. Actually, while Newberry's was biting the dust, it also became obvious that Discovery 2000 was going to eat up the rest of Second Avenue as well. The Calder Furniture building, which adjoined Newberry's, was leveled at the same time, as was Loveman's former Store for the Home. Things were going to look very different to anyone who might have been away from the city for several years.

Just as the museum officials had been promising all along, though, one familiar sight was going to be preserved no matter what: the corner clock. Renovated, it was restored to its proper location just days before the museum's grand opening on July 11, 1998. On that hot grand opening day, the complex was not known as Discovery 2000, the name that had been attached to it since the project was first announced. The funds needed to complete the project had been donated by Birmingham's legendary McWane Foundation, and in appreciation, the science museum was renamed the McWane Science Center. Also, where Newberry's had formerly stood, instead of an Omnimax theater there was an IMAX theater, simply another trademark belonging to the same theater company.

At the McWane Science Center today, there are still vestiges of its former life, but one has to know where to look for them. The various interactive exhibits occupy all but the fourth floor; the former bargain basement probably least resembles itself, due to the fact that much of it is taken up with an aquarium for saltwater creatures and a re-created Alabama forest environment for freshwater denizens. (The rooftop rainforest, alas, has still never sprouted.) The fourth floor, despite what one might think, looks even less like its Loveman's days than the main exhibit areas. Because of mold, mildew, asbestos and other unhealthy substances that thrived during the building's long vacancy, everything on that level remains stripped down to the bare concrete. Awaiting a decision on how to best display them permanently are some physical pieces of Loveman's that were saved, including the red and green up-and-down indicators from the elevators. Even the device that made their distinctive "ding" sound has been preserved in the hope that someday visitors may be able to press a button and hear it again. Also scattered throughout the warehoused artifacts are a few of the stone lions that once lined the rooftop of Saks/Melancon's/Newberry's.

While renovations were underway, crews found additional relics in what was formerly the advertising department and the sign shop. Many original ad layouts and other such remnants are carefully stored and rarely handled, befitting their status as fragile ghosts of the past.

In some areas, McWane has brought them back closer to the way they were in 1935 than they appeared on the day the store closed. Photographs taken soon after the city acquired the building show that the walls around the elevators had, at some point, been covered with what looks like carpet, a dark green color to match Loveman's standard logo. Today, the avocado surfacing has been stripped away to reveal the fine marble that existed underneath. Likewise, even though the original entrance bays are no longer used—doorways designed in the mid-1930s could not come close to meeting modern-day standards for handicapped access—they have been left in their original form as emergency exits, should

In many ways, the McWane Center renovation resulted in Loveman's looking better than it had in the store's last days. The top photo shows the ground-floor elevators as they were when the museum first acquired the building; the bottom photo shows the same spot today, with the dark green wall covering removed and the beautiful original 1935 marble exposed. *Bruce Brasseale collection.*

the need arise. They, too, retain their beautiful marble surroundings, and inside each foyer or vestibule, the marble shields bearing the intertwined "LJL" letters pay silent tribute to the store's three founders.

While on the subject, it might be just as well to take a brief glimpse at the eventual fate of Loveman's five branch stores. As we have seen, two of them were converted into Pizitz outlets and later remained part of the gang when McRae's bought out the Pizitz family. After McRae's own demise, the Western Hills Mall building became a Burlington Coat Factory; the Century Plaza outlet was abandoned even before the rest of the mall shut down in 2009.

In Bessemer, when Loveman's vacated downtown in 1968, its building became a Pizitz Budget Store. Pizitz subsequently closed that location in 1978 to set up shop at West Lake Mall, and the building (which, as we have seen, was already old when Loveman's moved in) has since been demolished. As for the former Loveman's at West Lake Mall, since Pizitz obviously did not need two locations in the same complex, after 1980 it served as home to a variety of stores before being shuttered like the rest of West Lake. The Huntsville Loveman's had a different fate: while the remainder of its home, The Mall, was demolished to make way for other developments, the Loveman's building stood its ground. As of the time of this writing, it was enjoying a second life as a Books-A-Million.

The saddest fate of all awaited the Loveman's at the Normandale shopping center in Montgomery. That neighborhood had fallen into a state

Of all the former Loveman's branch stores, none has met a sadder end than the one in Montgomery's Normandale shopping center. These March 2011 views show the decaying main floor and the top-level display window where Santa Claus once greeted kids. *Author's collection.*

of urban decay even outclassing any of the Birmingham locations, so once Loveman's had left the building, things rapidly went straight downhill. For a brief time, the structure housed a discount store and still later was used as offices and storage for the state's birth and death records. Today it sits in a decayed condition, choked by mold and mildew. A layer of grime several inches thick covers the once-proud main floor, but scraping away some of this grout reveals that the much-touted specks of black marble remain embedded in the terrazzo floors underneath. There seem to be no viable plans for resuscitating this cadaverous Loveman's.

Back in Birmingham, although occasionally a McWane Science Center article or a press release will refer to its building's heritage, naturally the reputation of Loveman's has been allowed to fade somewhat as the general public is further and further removed from it timewise. Obviously, anyone younger than their late thirties can have only the vaguest memories of the great department store, and considering how long downtown was in its retail tailspin, it is more likely that they would have to be older than that to remember it in its prime.

For many years after the 1980 closing, it was the former employees who did the most to keep Loveman's memory alive. As they died off, so did those memories. There were regular monthly get-togethers of the ex-employees until it was no longer practical to continue; today, those who remain see each other on more irregular and private occasions. In late 2011, several of them gathered to celebrate Del "Twinkles" Chambordon's ninetieth birthday, including Jerry Sklar, the only living former store president.

Perhaps it is best to let one of those former employees deliver our benediction here. Preserved in one of Del Chambordon's scrapbooks was a typewritten poem by Ann Helms, late of the Loveman's stationery department. Her simple but heartfelt verses read like a eulogy, as well they might:

> It's nice to meet with old friends
> And chatter all day long,
> With thoughts caught up in laughter
> That fills our hearts with song.
>
> We recall our first assignment
> At Loveman's store of great renown.
> Some tell of a quiet life of retirement
> While others speak of new jobs they have found.

In November 2011, there was a reunion of Del "Twinkles" Chambordon and Jerry Sklar, the last living Loveman's president, at Twinkles's ninetieth birthday party. *Author's collection.*

To some we pour out our sorrow,
Telling of loved ones gone on before.
Gratefully we tell of our new infant darling;
God has His way to even the score.

Our mother store was the finest of all structures,
Well known throughout the whole U.S.A.
Our very aim, to make her the greatest
As we faithfully toiled from day to day.

Her doors are now closed forever,
Each went their sad and separate ways;
Sweet, warm memories will always linger
At our luncheon get-together every thirty days.

Why don't you make it a point to go down to the McWane Science Center and meet someone under the clock sometime soon? It's still there waiting for you.

BIBLIOGRAPHY

BOOKS

Atkins, Leah Rawls. *The Valley and the Hills: An Illustrated History of Birmingham and Jefferson County*. Woodland Hills, CA: Windsor Publications, 1981.

Century Plus: A Bicentennial Portrait of Birmingham, Alabama. Birmingham: Oxmoor Press, 1976.

Hollis, Tim. *Birmingham Broadcasting*. Charleston, SC: Arcadia Publishing, 2006.

————. *Birmingham's Theater and Retail District*. Charleston, SC: Arcadia Publishing, 2005.

————. *Pizitz: Your Store*. Charleston, SC: The History Press, 2010.

————. *Vintage Birmingham Signs*. Charleston, SC: Arcadia Publishing, 2007.

Illustrated Souvenir of Birmingham's $3,000,000 Fire. Compiled and issued for the benefit of the Birmingham Firemen's Relief Association, 1934.

Jenkins, Carol, and Elizabeth Gardner Hines. *Black Titan: A.G. Gaston and the Making of a Black American Millionaire*. New York: Ballantine, 2005.

King, Pamela Sterne. *50 Years and Counting: A History of Operation New Birmingham*. Birmingham: Operation New Birmingham, 2008.

Laughin, Jerry W. *Bama Burning: Fourteen Famous Fires in Alabama*. N.p.: self-published, 1974.

McMillan, Malcolm C. *Yesterday's Birmingham*. Miami: E.A. Seemann Publishing, 1975.

O'Donnell, Joe. *The Forge: Metal to Medicine*. Birmingham: Regional Chamber of Commerce, 2007.

Portrait of Birmingham. Birmingham: Birmingham Centennial Corporation, 1971.

White, Marjorie Longenecker. *Downtown Birmingham*. Birmingham: Birmingham Historical Society, 1977.

NEWSPAPER AND MAGAZINE ARTICLES

Archibald, John. "City Buys Newberry Site for Science Museum Facility." *Birmingham News*, April 14, 1992.

Beiman, Irving. "Big New Britt's Opens Downtown." December 3, 1962.

————. "400 Car Garage Opening Monday." *Birmingham News*, November 14, 1971.

————. "Long-Awaited Mall Begun in Bessemer." October 15, 1968.

————. "Loveman's Charts Huge Rebuilding." October 1, 1967.

————. "Loveman's Store in Mall to Replace Bessemer Unit." October 17, 1968.

————. "Loveman's to Build in Big New Center." July 17, 1966.

————. "Mayor Hopefuls Cut Ribbon." May 22, 1961.

————. "6th Loveman's 'Complete Store.'" August 3, 1975.

————. "Sklar Is New President of Loveman's." March 15, 1978.

————. "Work Begins on Western Hills Mall." November 8, 1967.

Bell, Elma. "Historic Home Gets New Lease on a New Life." *Birmingham News*, September 16, 1984.

Birmingham News. "A.B. Loveman Is Dead at His Home on the Southside." July 4, 1916.

————. "Alabama Men Build New Loveman Store of Alabama Material." August 12, 1935.

————. "Atlanta Man to Take Over Loveman's." September 11, 1964.

————. "Bessemer Welcomes Loveman's Opening." March 30, 1954.

————. "Big $850,000 Expansion Is Planned by Loveman's." August 30, 1944.

————. "Birmingham Offers to Help Loveman's Find Buyer for Store." March 6, 1980.

————. "Boutwell Warns 'Outside Agitators.'" April 4, 1963.

————. "Breyer Now Veep of City Stores Co." July 18, 1965.

————. "Civic Leaders Join Hands to Push Birmingham Green." January 4, 1971.

———. "Color Ads Win National Award for Loveman's." April 5, 1959.

———. "Courage to 'Come Back' Is Only a Chapter in Romance of Merchant's Life." April 9, 1934.

———. Editorial, "Joe Loveman Retires as Department Store Head." August 21, 1931.

———. Editorial, "Joseph H. Loveman." March 1, 1951.

———. Editorial, "Loveman's Closing." April 3, 1980.

———. Editorial, "Opening of the New Home of Loveman, Joseph & Loeb." November 19, 1935.

———. "Flames Take $3,000,000 Toll in Downtown Business Area." March 11, 1934.

———. "Greater and Finer Loveman's to Open Doors Wednesday." November 19, 1935.

———. "John Breyer Quitting May 1 as President of Loveman's." March 23, 1972.

———. "Joseph Loveman, Department Store Executive, Dies." February 28, 1951.

———. "L, J & L Are to Build Big Annex to Present Store." July 3, 1916.

———. "L, J & L Store to Keep Individuality." August 15, 1925.

———. "Loveman Is Made Director of City Stores Company." January 14, 1932.

———. "Loveman, Joseph & Loeb Observes Fiftieth Year as Department Store." May 2, 1937.

———. "Loveman's Announces New Building Plans." August 21, 1934.

———. "Loveman's Appoints Sklar Vice President." April 17, 1971.

———. "Loveman's Begins Seven-Story Deck." April 20, 1970.

———. "Loveman's New President Has ideas, Dynamism." May 4, 1972.

———. "Loveman's One of 8 U.S. Retailers Honored for Excellence by Magazine." March 7, 1976.

———. "Loveman's President to Head City Stores' New Orleans Outlets." March 28, 1980.

———. "Loveman's Put Seven Moving Stairways into Operation." September 28, 1955.

———. "Loveman's to Open Branch Store in Huntsville Thursday." March 2, 1966.

———. "Loveman's to Open West Lake Store." October 28, 1969.

———. "Loveman Store Here 42 Years." Undated clipping, 1929.

———. "Loveman Store Open to Public after Big Fire." March 28, 1934.

———. "Loveman Store Order Placed." February 25, 1935.

————. "Loveman's West Opening Tomorrow." March 10, 1970.

————. "Loveman's Will Establish New Store in Montgomery's Normandale Area." April 19, 1953.

————. "Loveman's Will Reopen for Sale." April 26, 1980.

————. "M.V. Joseph, Pioneer Merchant, Dies after Several Weeks Illness." May 5, 1929.

————. "O.W. Schanbacher, Loveman's Head, Dies." September 18, 1960.

————. "Paul Dowd Heads Loveman's Stores." May 2, 1961.

————. "Police Subdue Pickets; Lunch Counters Mix." July 30, 1963.

————. "Quarter of a Million." March 14, 1899.

————. "Romance of Birmingham Man Ends in Tragedy." November 1, 1917.

————. "Shoppers, Clerks Routed as Smoke Fills Structure." March 10, 1934.

————. "Thousands Attend Loveman's Opening in Huntsville." March 4, 1966.

————. "23,000 Visit Loveman's New Store." June 21, 1949.

Birmingham Post. "Loveman's Opens New 5-Story Annex." June 20, 1949.

Birmingham Post-Herald. "Loveman's Opens Store in Bessemer." March 30, 1954.

————. "Loveman's Plans Fairfield Store." July 18, 1966.

————. "Loveman's Will Stay Open until 8:30 on Monday Nights." January 1, 1953.

Carter, Lane. "Miss O'Sullivan in Town for Fashion Commentator Role." *Birmingham News*, February 15, 1967.

Cummins, Don. "Expansion by Loveman's Is Announced." *Birmingham Post-Herald*, December 2, 1965.

Edge, Lynn. "Santa Visits for Breakfast and Ice Cream." *Birmingham News*, undated clipping.

Frieden, Kitty. "Loveman's Eyed as New Headquarters for Police." *Birmingham News*, April 11, 1980.

Gordon, Tom. "Remembering Downtown." *Birmingham News*, May 12, 1991

Hargrove, Thomas. "Loveman's Expected to Close This Month." April 1, 1980.

————. "Loveman's Sale Considered." *Birmingham Post-Herald*, February 20, 1980.

————. "Negotiators Hold Fate of Loveman's." *Birmingham Post-Herald*, March 28, 1980.

————. "700 Loveman's Workers to Be Jobless Next Week." *Birmingham Post-Herald*, April 3, 1980.

———. "Two Loveman's Stores at Malls Sold to Pizitz." *Birmingham Post-Herald*, April 12, 1980.

Kaimann, Frederick. "A $50 Million Downtown Dream." *Birmingham News*, December 1, 1993.

Kepple, David. "Rainy Day Story." *Birmingham News*, April 4, 1980.

Lewis, Danny. "Closing of Loveman's Brings End to Woman's 'Family Store' Career." *Montgomery Advertiser*, April 6, 1980.

Monitor, Leigh Ann. "Old Loveman's Clock to Show Its Face Again." *Birmingham Post-Herald*, July 6, 1998.

Montgomery Advertiser. "Normandale Opening Tomorrow at 10 a.m." September 9, 1954.

New York Times. "Emil Loeb, a Founder of Birmingham Store." June 20, 1941.

———. "Soldier Leaps to Death." November 1, 1917.

Raabe, Nancy. "Like Looking Back in Time: Loveman's Clock." *Birmingham News*, July 7, 1998.

Shook, Phil R. "Loveman's Fate May Be Determined by May." *Birmingham News*, February 21, 1980.

———. "Loveman's Stores Either Will Be Sold or Closed This Month." April 1, 1980.

———. "The Loveman's Years." April 3, 1980.

Teague, Sarah. "Starr Shines at Fashion-Luncheon Presented by Linly Heflin-Loveman's." *Birmingham Post-Herald*, September 18, 1970.

Underwood, Jerry. "City Oks $1.3 Million to Buy Loveman's for Science Center." *Birmingham News*, December 19, 1990.

———. "City Wants Old Loveman's for Museum." *Birmingham News*, December 16, 1990.

Washburn, Dennis. "Loveman's Works on Expansion Plan." *Birmingham News*, April 16, 1969.

———. "Ohio Store Exec New President of Loveman's." *Birmingham News*, February 1, 1977.

Williams, Roy. "Closing after 8 Decades." *Birmingham News*, January 25, 1995.

———. "Walls to Fall." *Birmingham News*, March 8, 1996.

ABOUT THE AUTHOR

Tim Hollis has been a pop culture historian literally all his life. He likes to tell how, when he was nine years old, he was writing letters to companies and trying to preserve the memories of things from when he was three years old. This mania for living in the past has resulted in twenty-one books (as of right now, anyway) ranging in subjects from southern tourism nostalgia to Birmingham history to children's television and children's records, among other topics. He also owns a museum of toys, advertising, holiday memorabilia and other baby boomer relics that he makes available to visitors and researchers by appointment. Having lived in Birmingham his entire life, he supplies the nostalgic materials for the popular www.BirminghamRewound.com website, through which he may also be contacted.

Visit us at
www.historypress.net